# WASHINGTON

*See it again for the first time*

## *Looking Up!*

For Norm & Libby —

Keep looking up!

Marty Lahr

Woolly Oxley was born in Findlay, Ohio.
He was part of the family of Mike, Pat and Chadd Oxley.
Woolly was an Old English Sheepdog.

I had been photographing the annual Christmas card for Congressman Oxley and his family for several years. Every year, each picture included Woolly.  When we decided to use the Supreme Court as a backdrop,Woolly was fourteen years old and severe arthritis limited his mobility. Because of Woolly's condition, the Oxleys were late. While waiting, I started to explore the building and realized I was looking at it from angles I had never noticed before. I decided to try out a new fisheye lens and shot two rolls of film before they arrived.

After developing the film I was intrigued by the shapes and designs I saw. I began to wonder what other buildings in Washington looked like,  "Looking Up."  For the next six weeks, every Sunday morning, I drove around the city looking, discovering, seeing Washington in a totally different way.  Although I had lived in the D.C. area for over twenty-five years, I was literally "Seeing It For The First Time".

After photographing over sixty locations, I made prints and asked my wife "Where are these buildings?"  Although she couldn't identify any, she said: "I really don't care where they are, I just love the colors, designs and artistry."

Unfortunately,
Woolly died a few months after the family photograph was taken.

Woolly, I'm sorry you were so uncomfortable that day, but if you had been on time, I wouldn't have looked up. I wouldn't have found these views of Washington. More important to me, without you, this book would never have happened.

Thanks Woolly

*Marty*

# Look Up, Washington

In the nation's capital, where you stand depends on where you sit.
Which side of the fence.  Which side of the aisle.

And what you see depends on where you look.  Whether you see the forest or the trees,
the macro view or the micro view, the scuffed floors or the skylights.

Photographer Marty LaVor has traveled the world, seeing what others missed, and bringing
his visions home so the rest of us could share his vision.  For this book, he trained his lens
and imaginative eye homeward and, in doing so, he gives Washingtonians a city we have
lived in and looked at but never seen before.

Even those of us who thought we knew all of the angles discover new ones with LaVor.

Why is it so important to see the sculpted domes and the vaulted ceilings of public places?
To be inside, outside or upside down in familiar spaces?  LaVor believes that perspective
shapes perception.  Walk a mile behind LaVor's lens and you'll see wonders where once
you saw only mortar and monuments, steel and stone.

So look up Washington!

*LESLIE MILK-Lifestyle Editor-Washingtonian magazine*

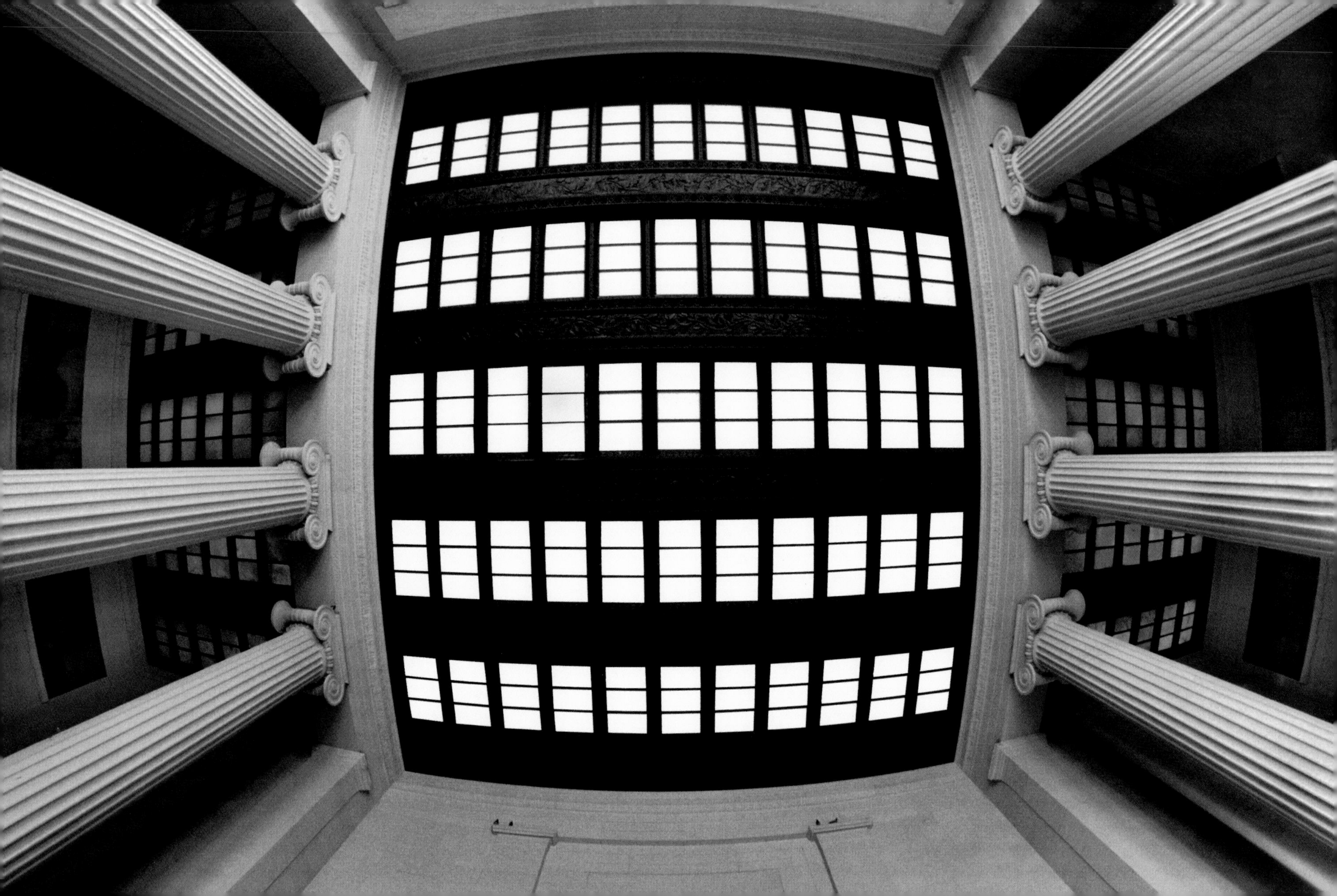

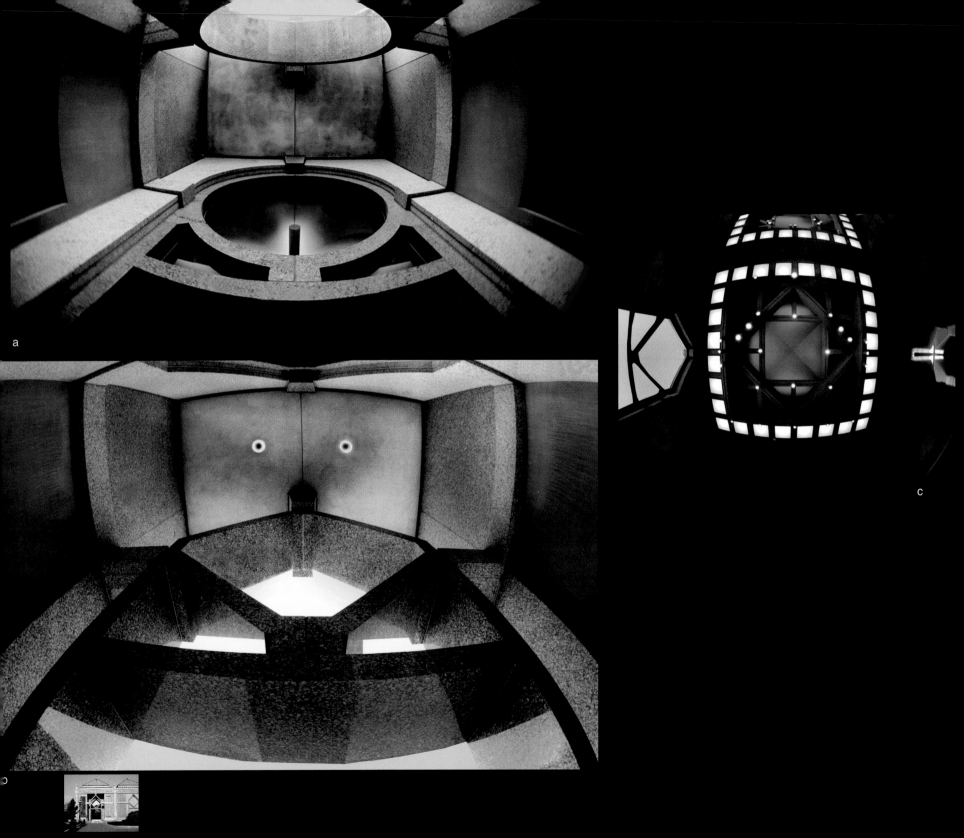

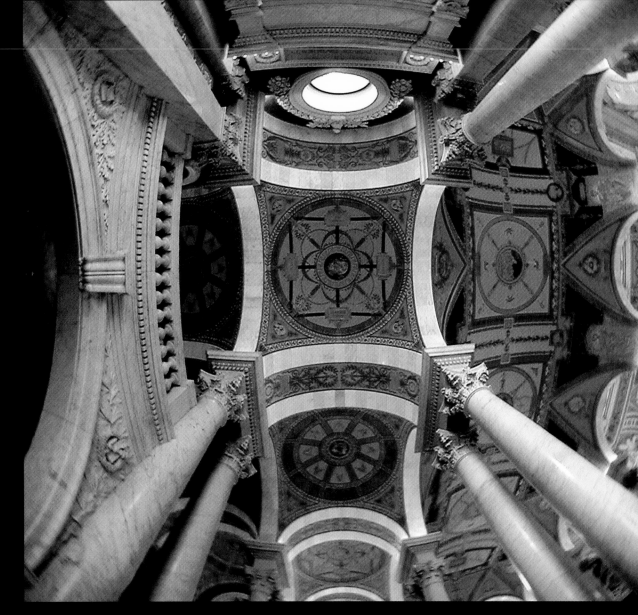

Library of Congress (outside & inside)

b

Hart Senate Office Building (c)

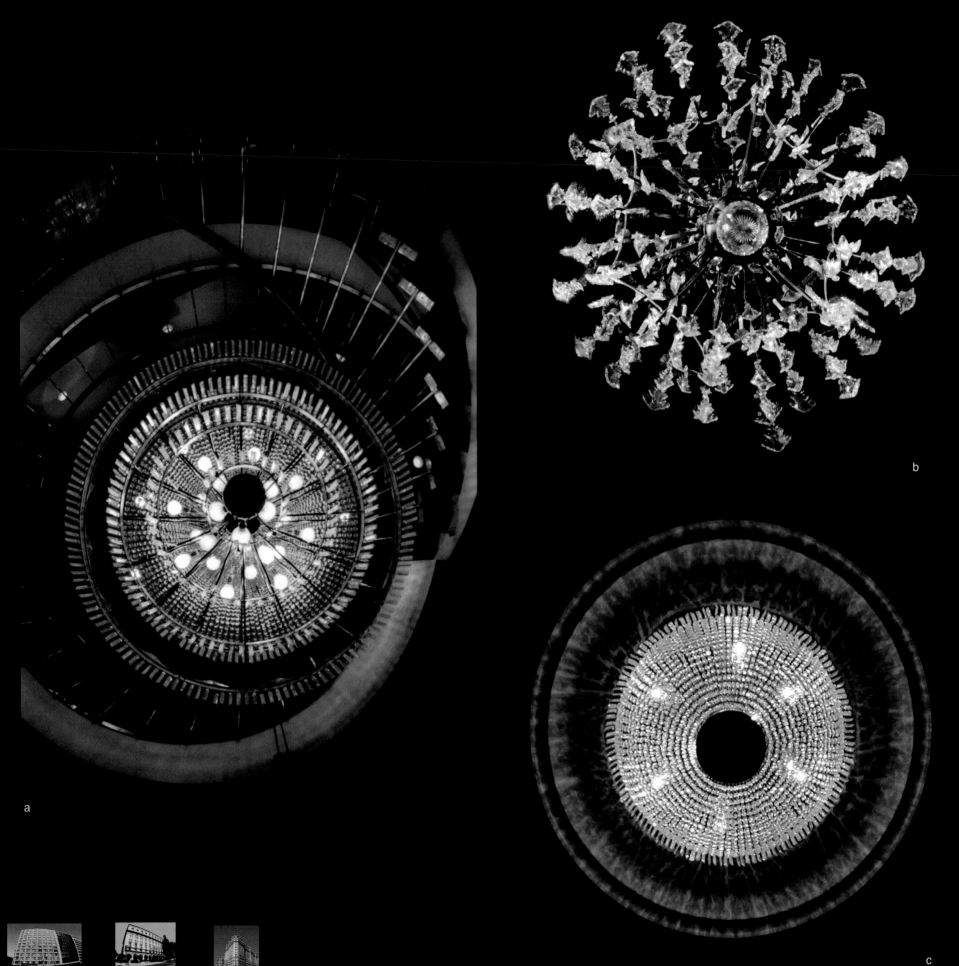

The Madison (a)    The St. Regis (b)    The Willard (c)

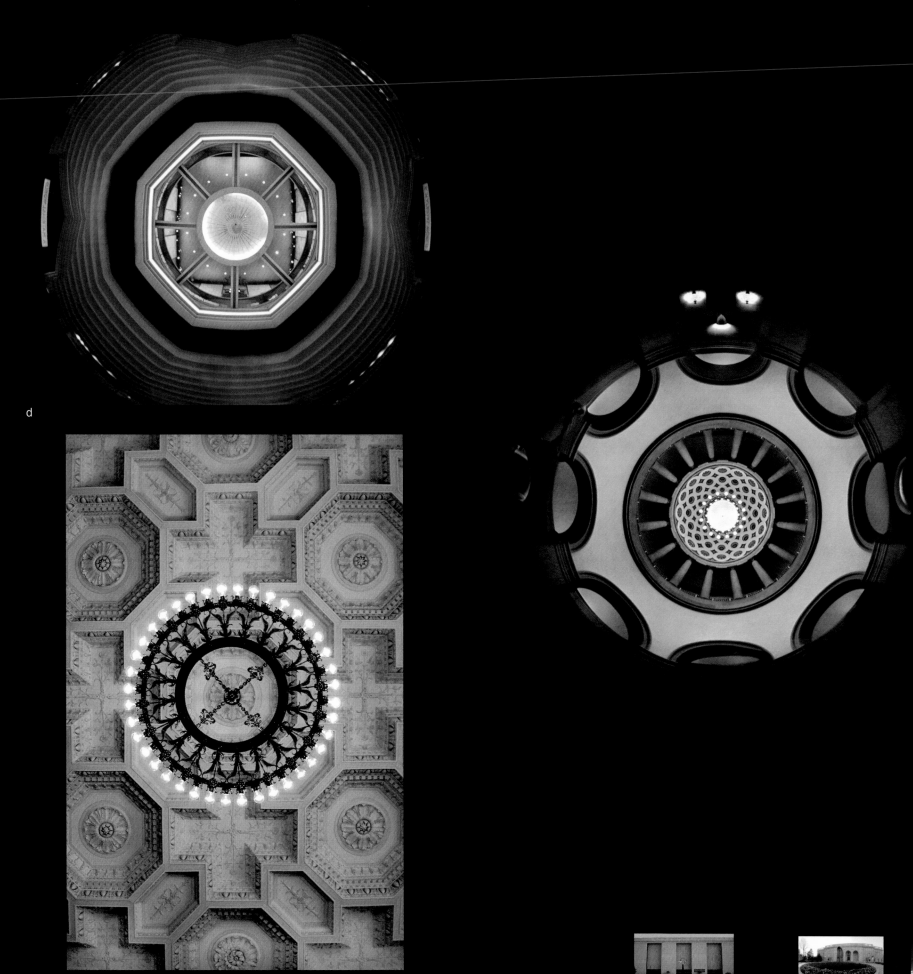

National Museum of American History (d)    Freer Gallery (e)    U.S. Capitol (f)

Smithsonian Arts & Industries Building

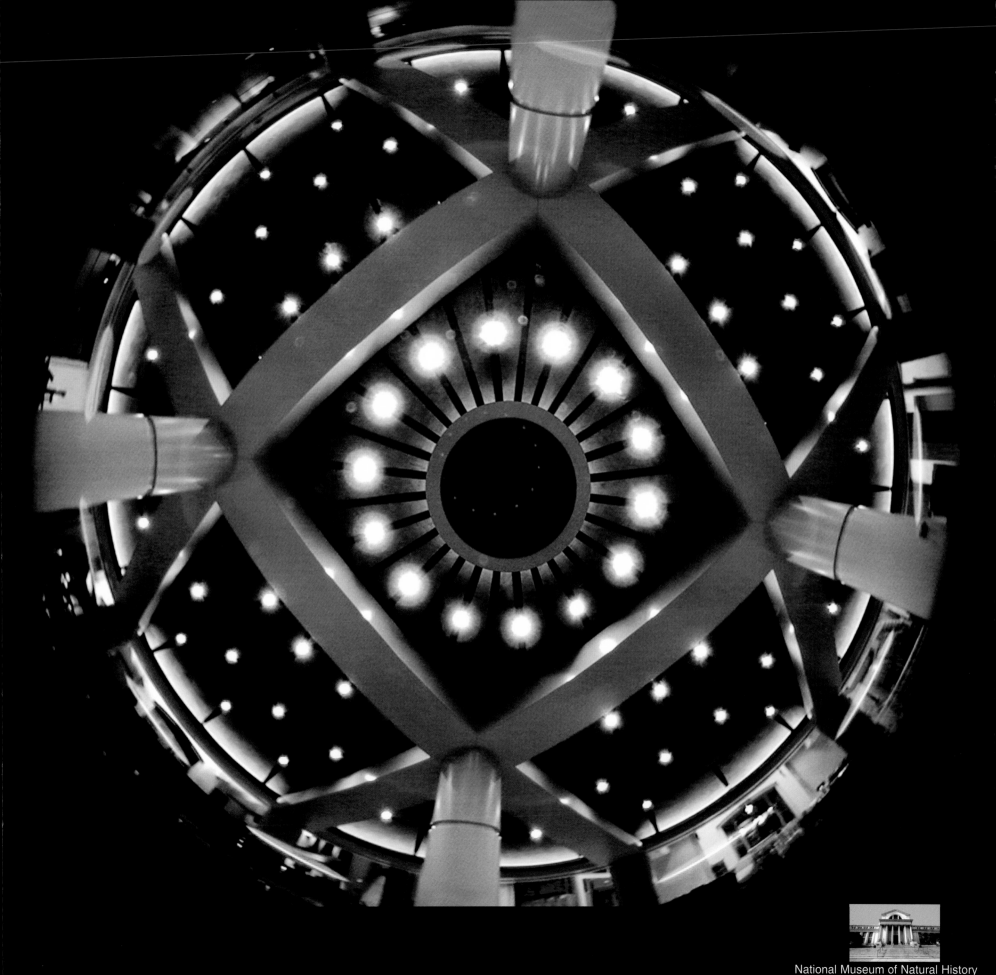

American Medical Association (a)    Washington National Cathedral (b)

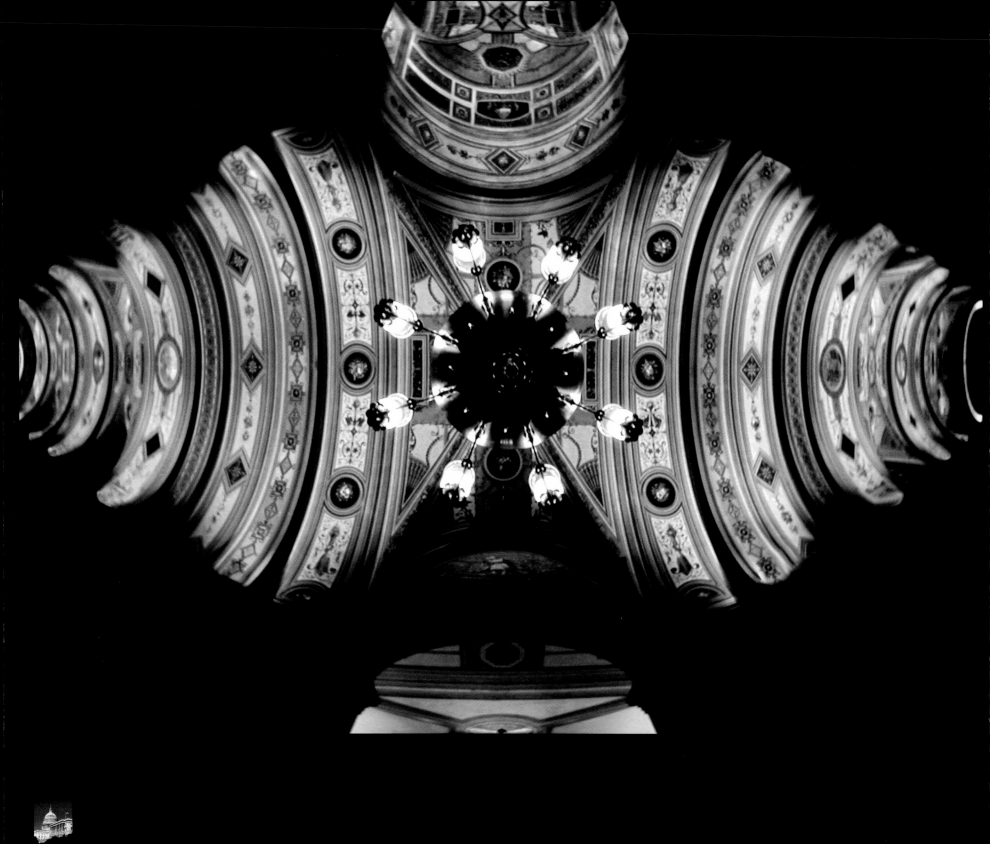

U.S. Capitol

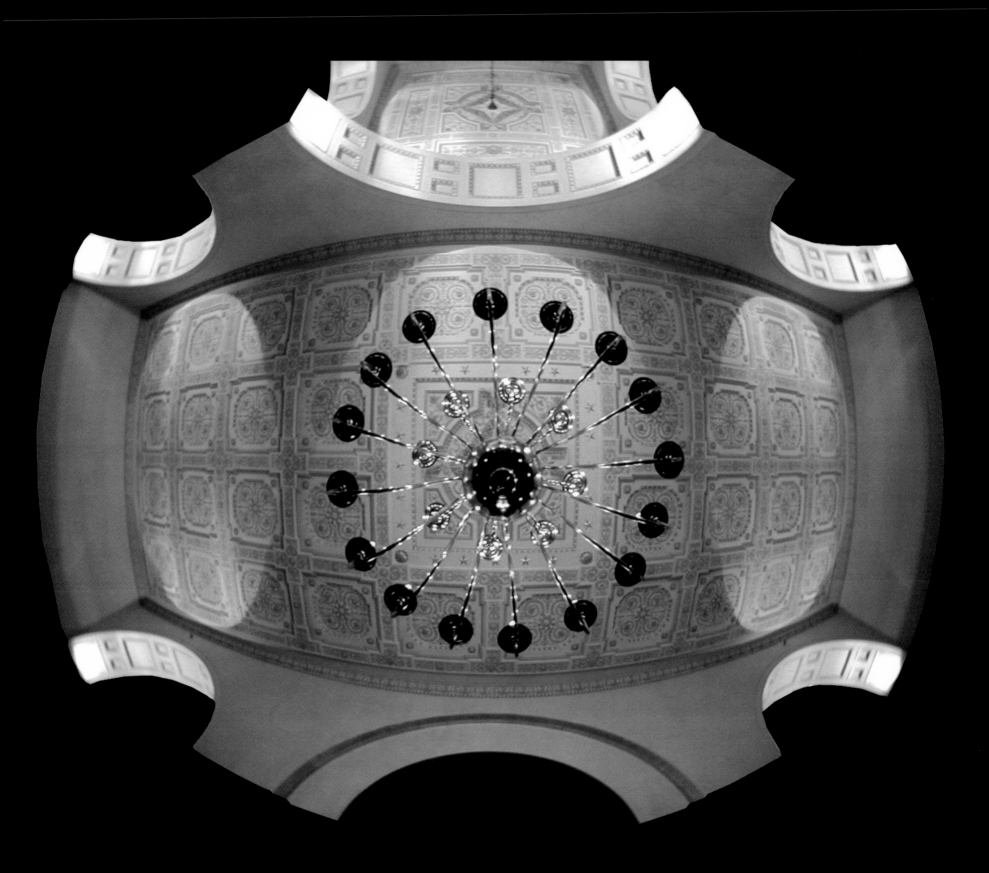

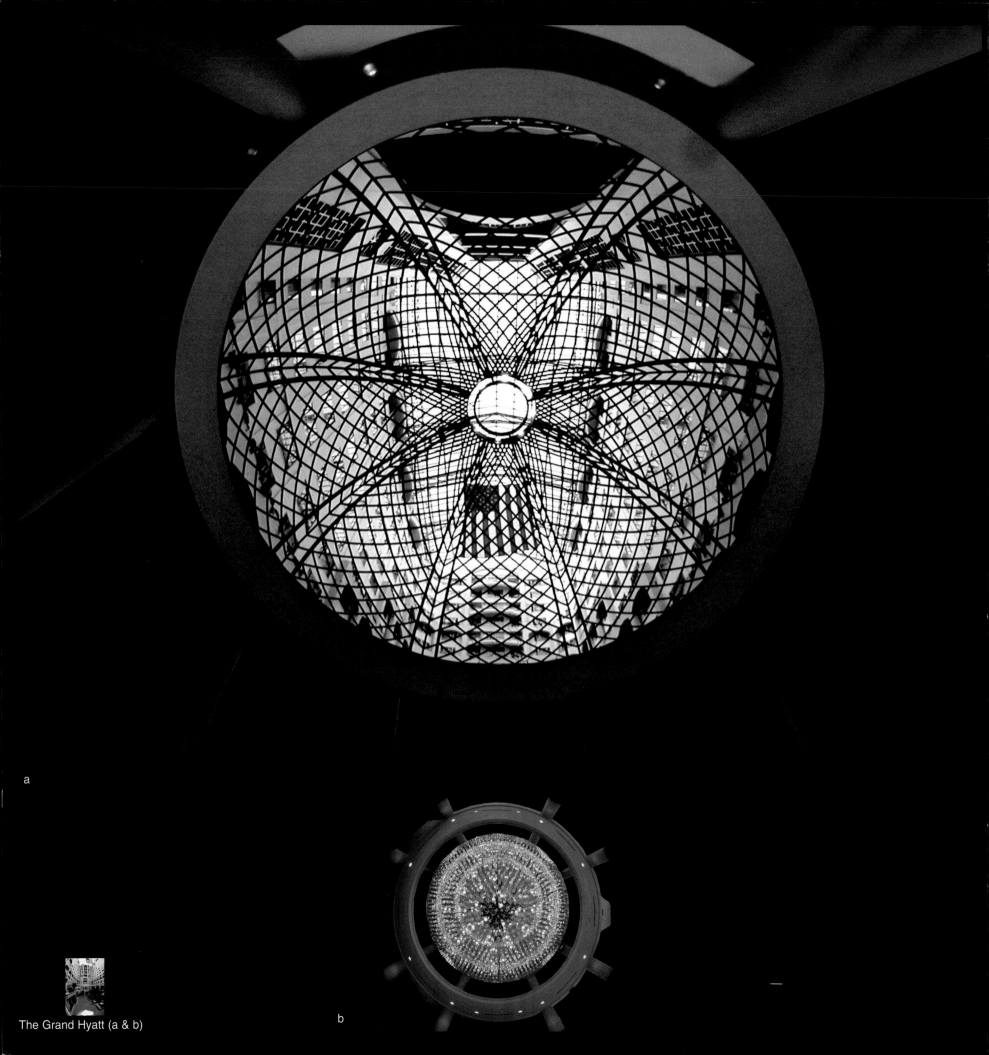

The Grand Hyatt (a & b)

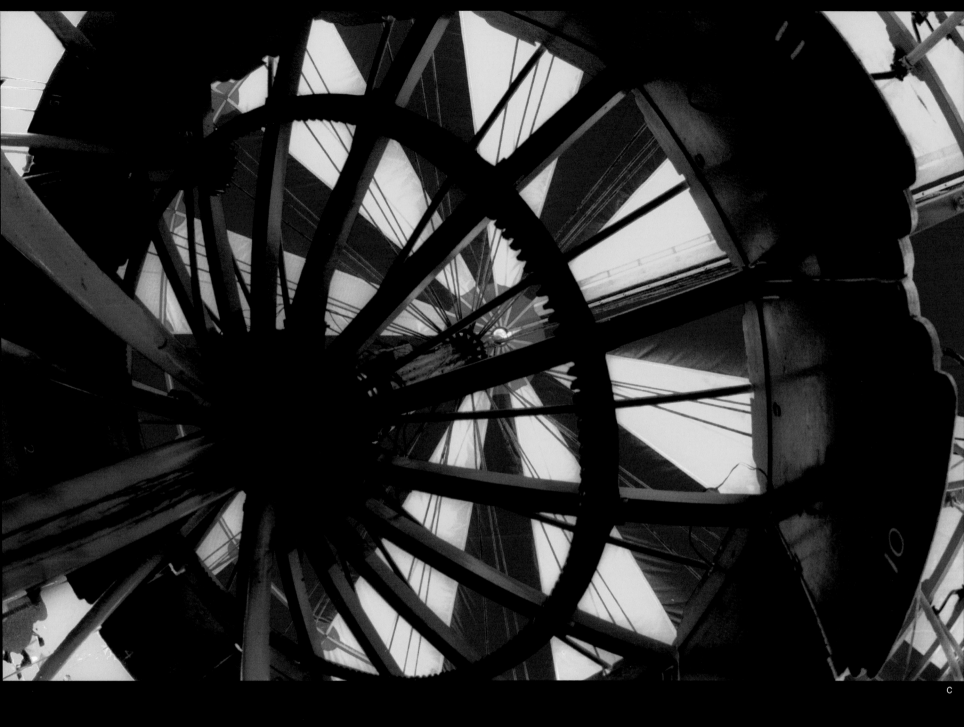

c

Smithsonian Merry-Go-Round (c

Department of Housing & Urban Development

a

National Association of Broadcasters (a)

b

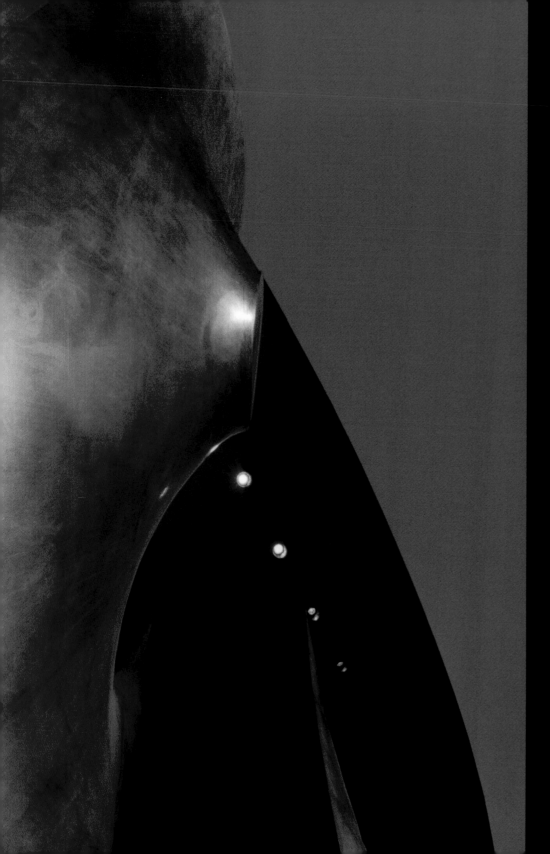

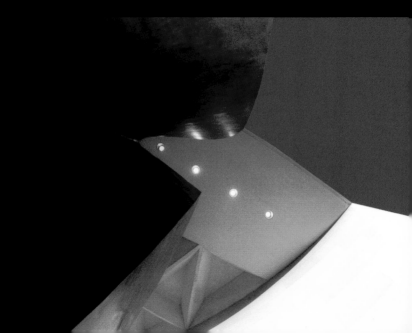

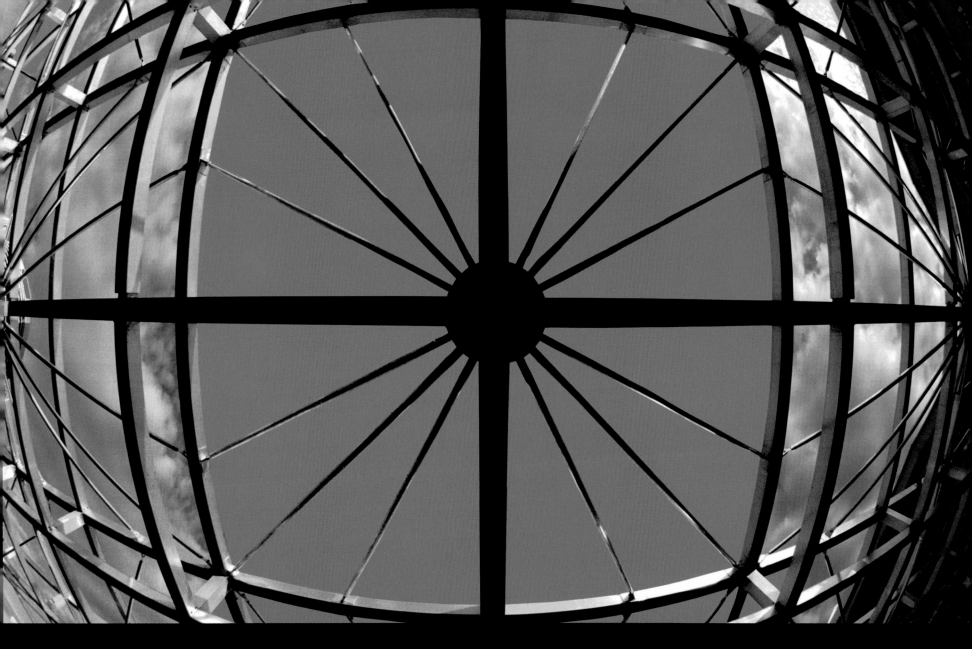

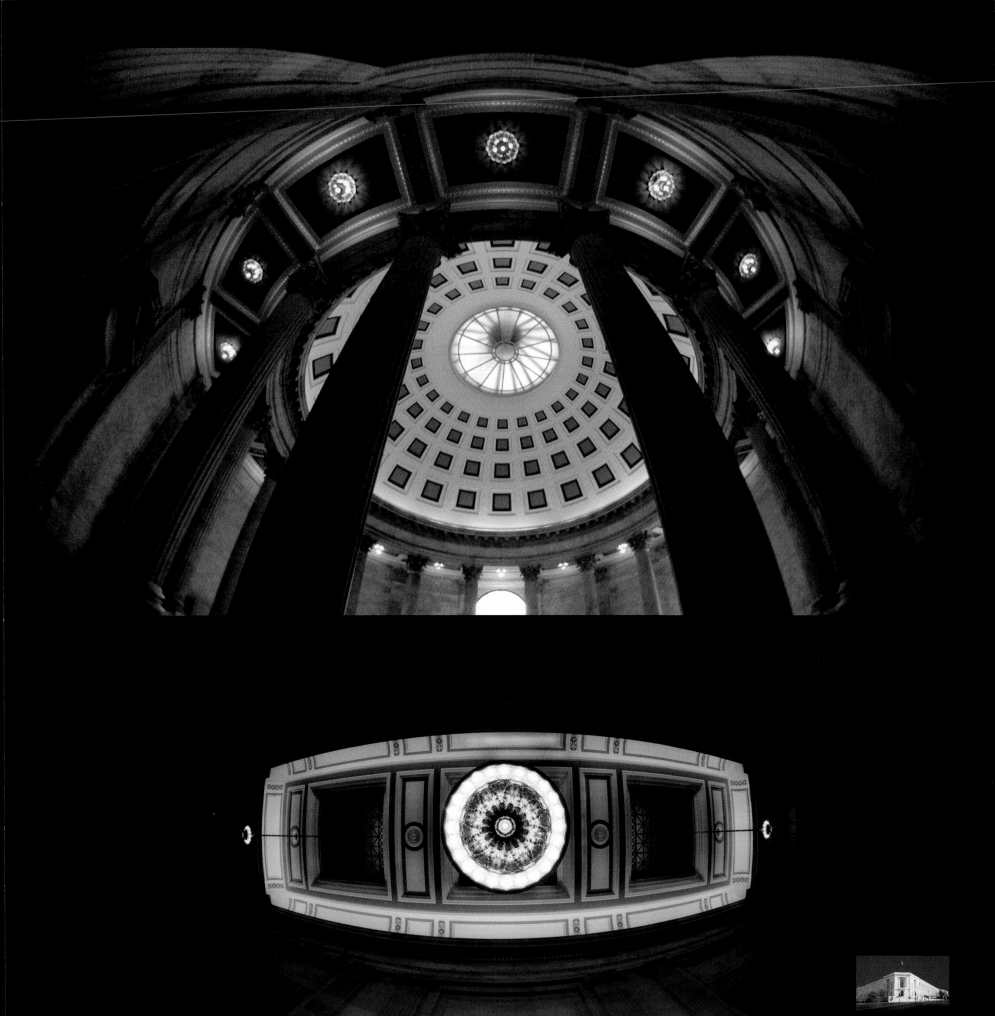

Russell Senate Office Building

National Shrine of the Immaculate Conception (a & b)

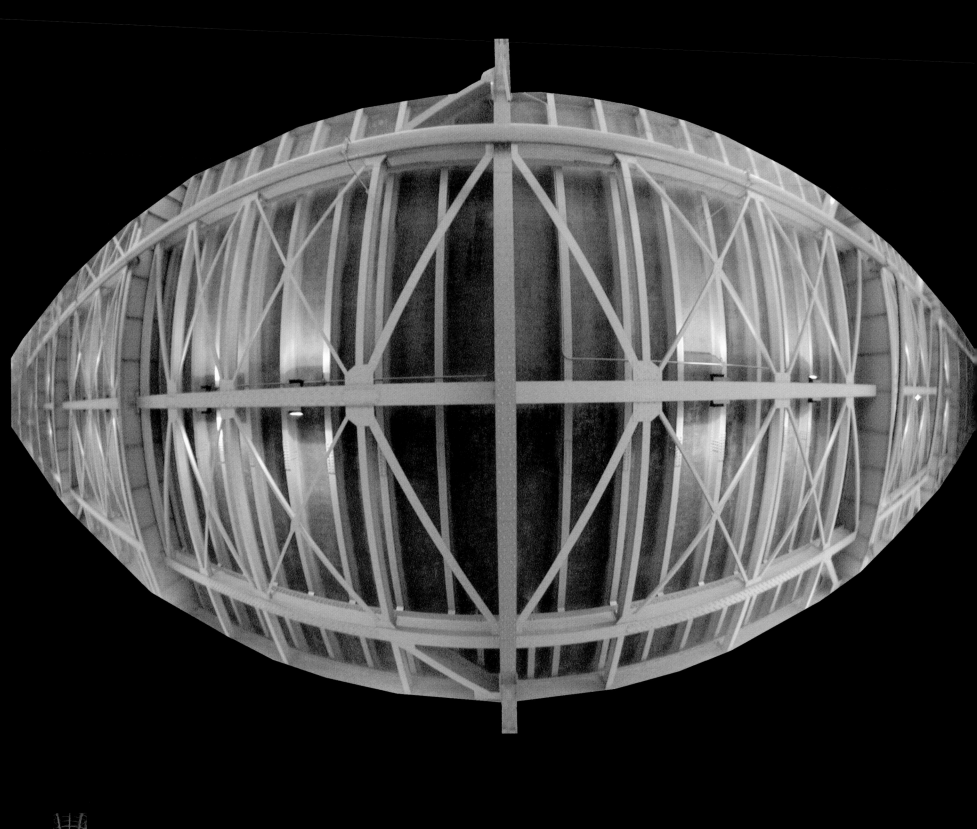

Whitehurst Freeway

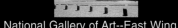

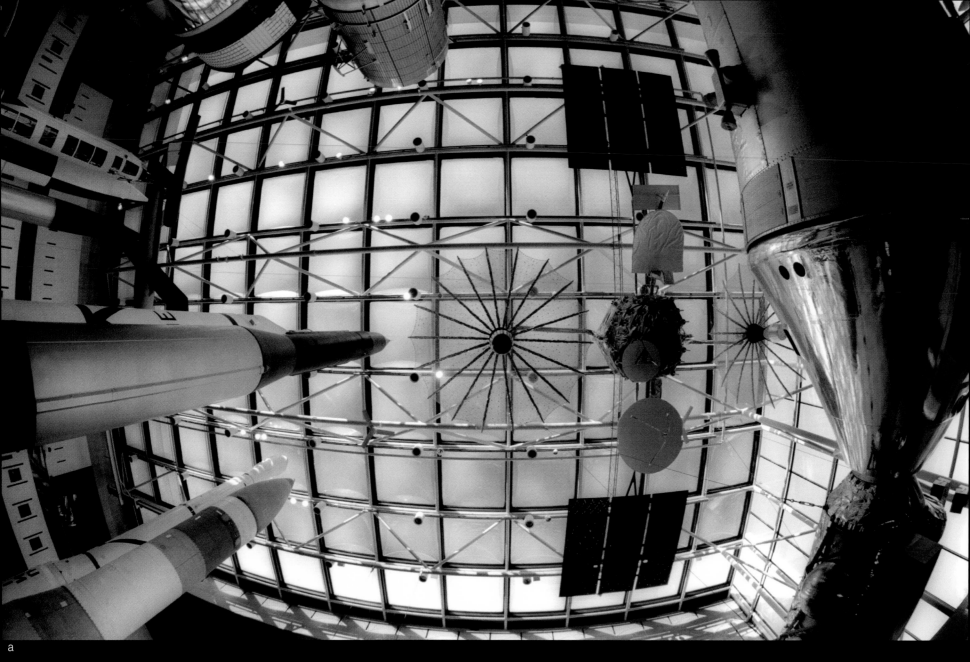

a

b

National Museum for Air & Space (a)

National Postal Museum (b)

The Mayflower (c)

Frank D. Reeves Center (d)

a

b

Library of Congress-Madison Building (a)

Washington Hilton (b)   American History Museum (c)

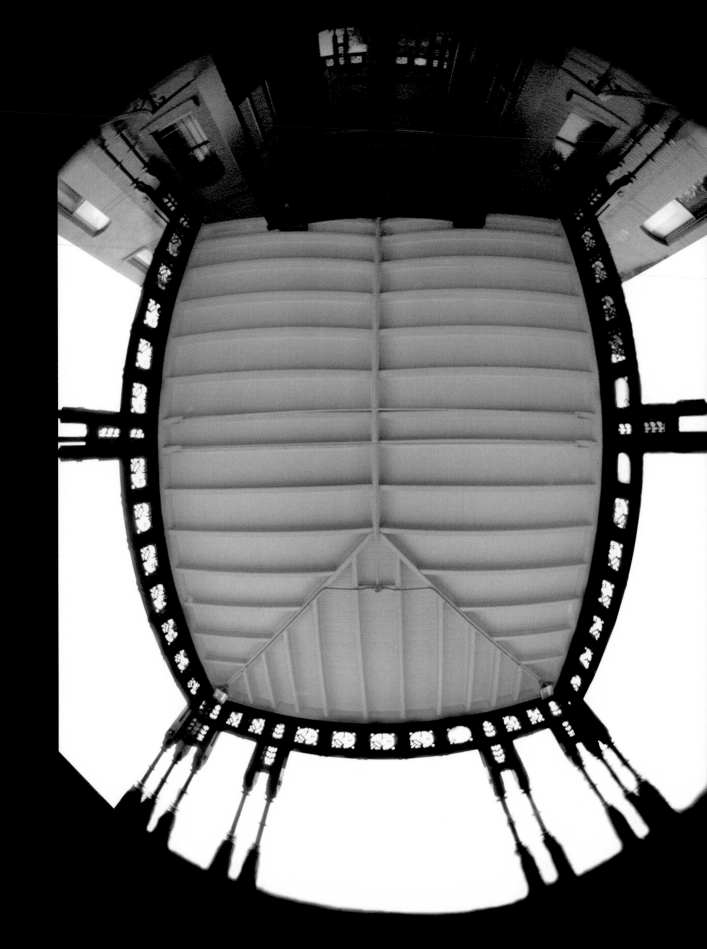

b

a

Washington National Cathedral (a)

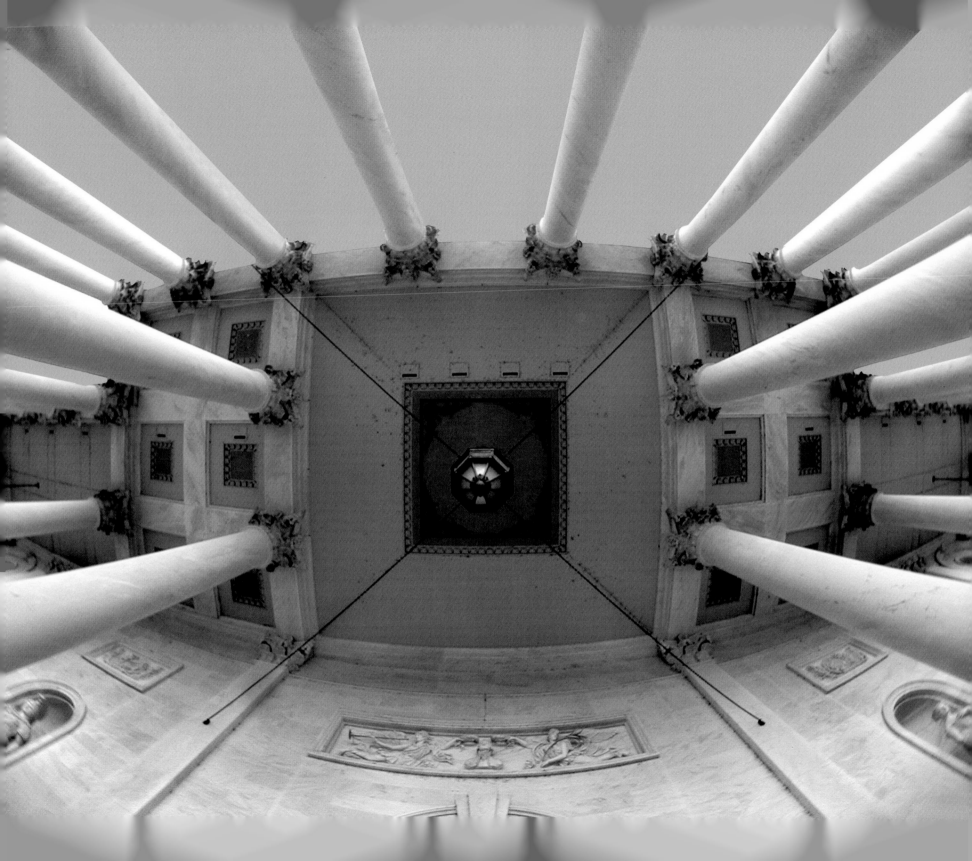

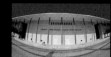

a

a

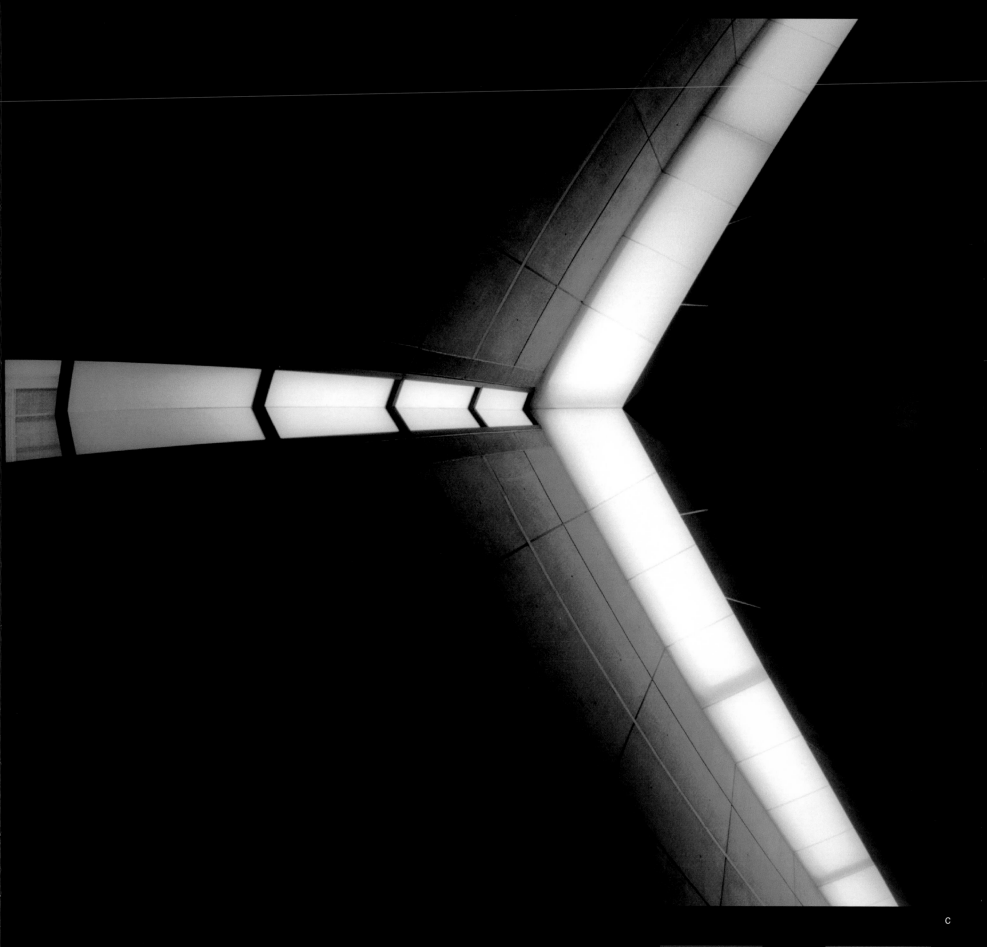

c

State Department (a)   Holocaust Memorial Museum (b & c)

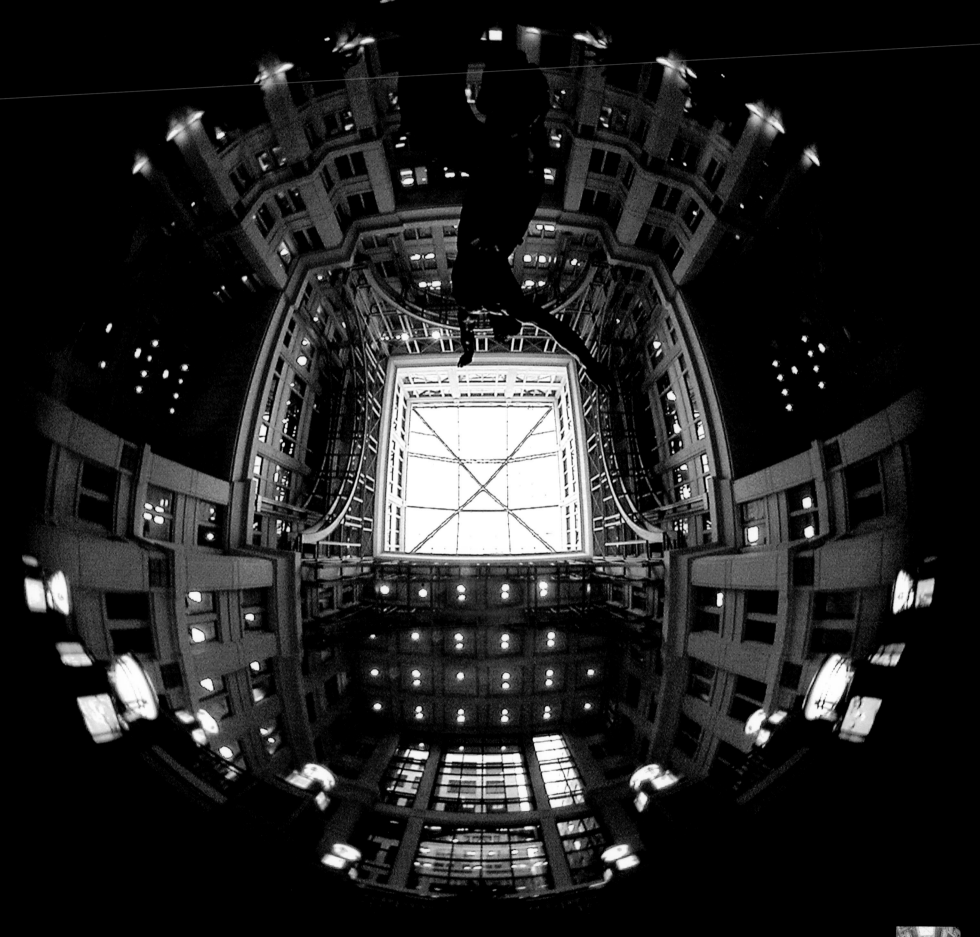

Homer Building

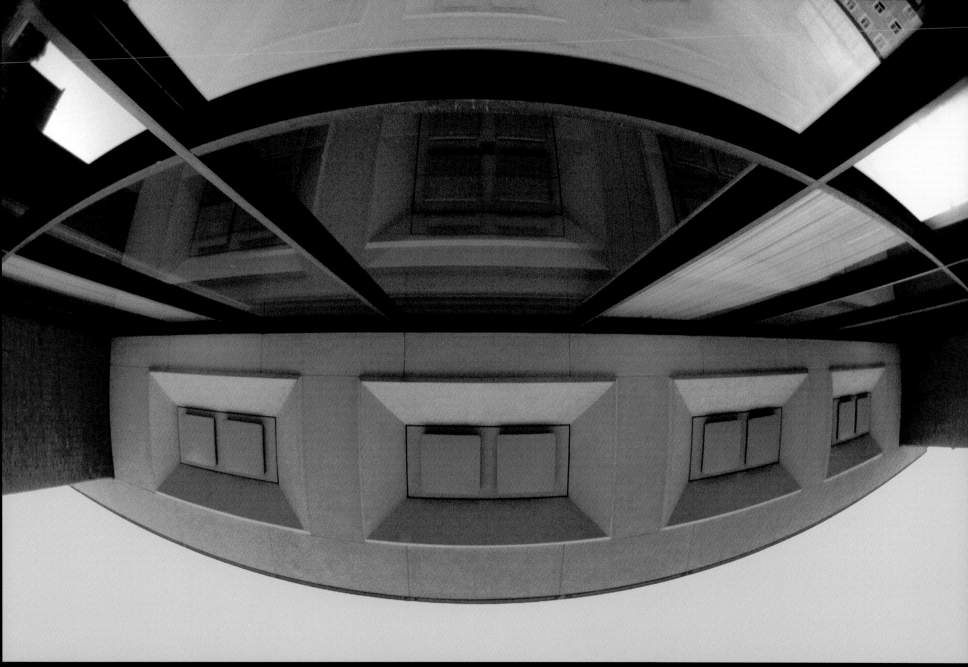

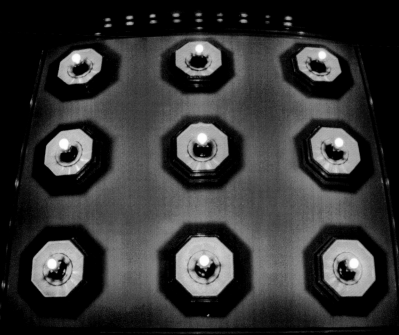

The Grand Hyatt

Union Station

Anderson House

2400 N Street NW

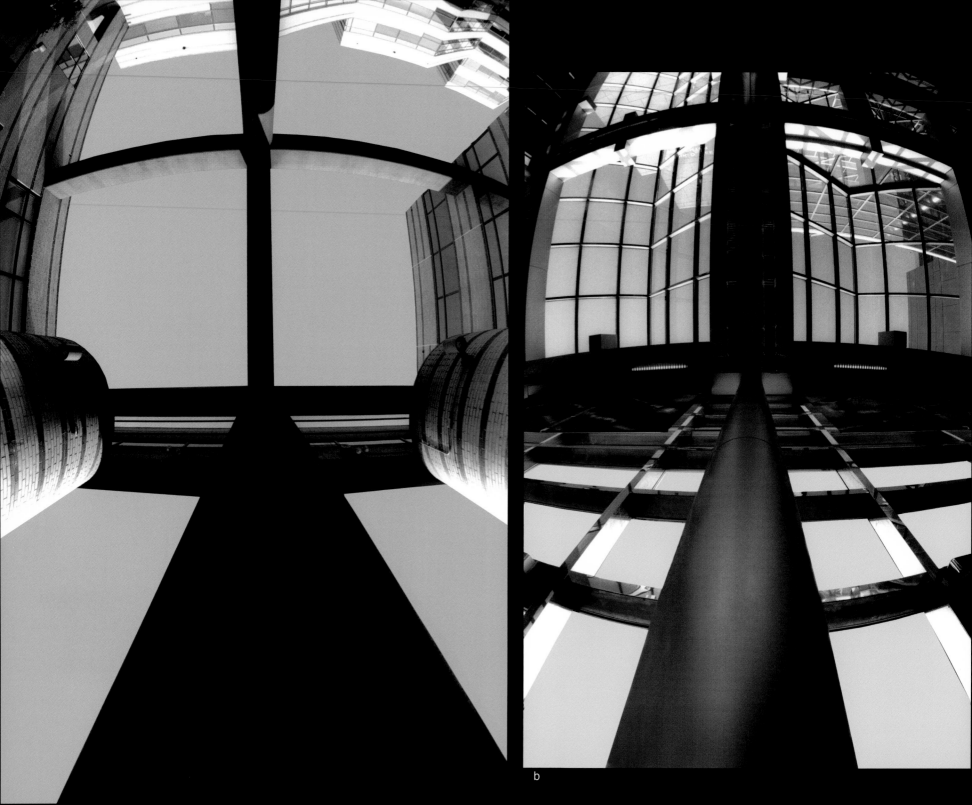

Van Ness Metro Station (a)   Frank D. Reeves Center (b)

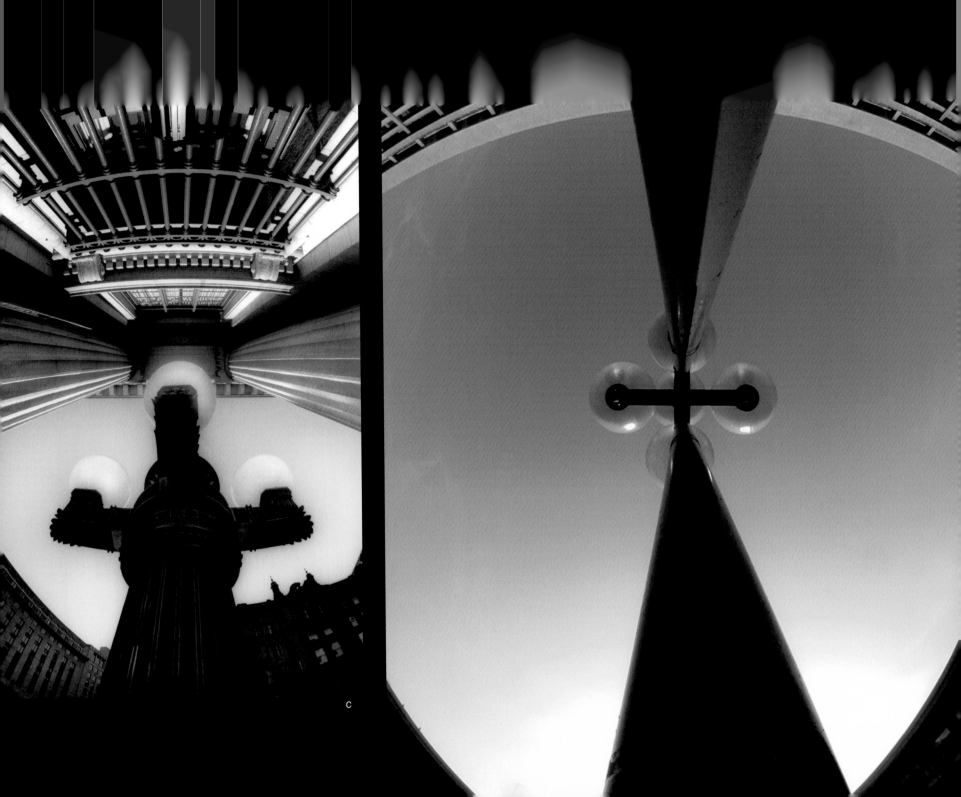

U. S. Supreme Court (night & day)

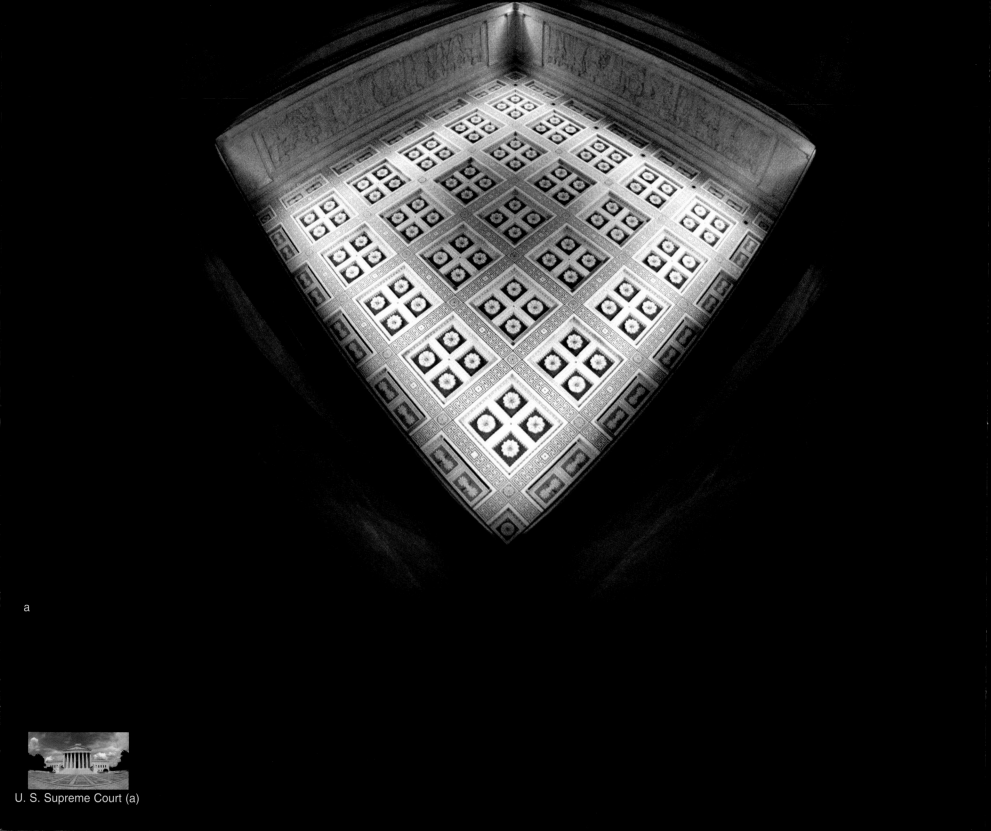

a

U. S. Supreme Court (a)

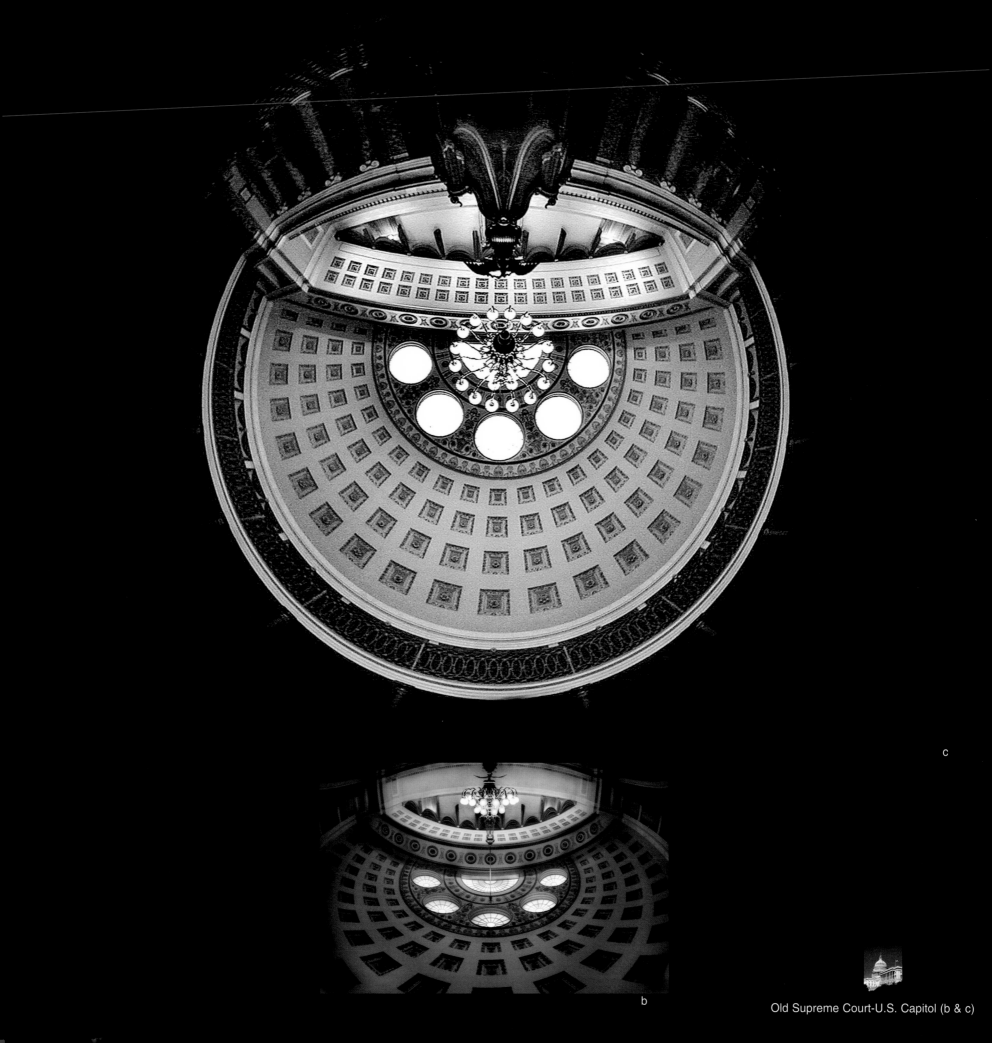

c

b

Old Supreme Court-U.S. Capitol (b & c)

a

b

 Cosmos Club (a)  Thurgood Marshall Federal Judiciary Building-(b)

a

b

1775 Pennsylvania Avenue NW (a & b)

World Health Organization

a

b

Federal Reserve-(a & b)

4th District Police Headquarters

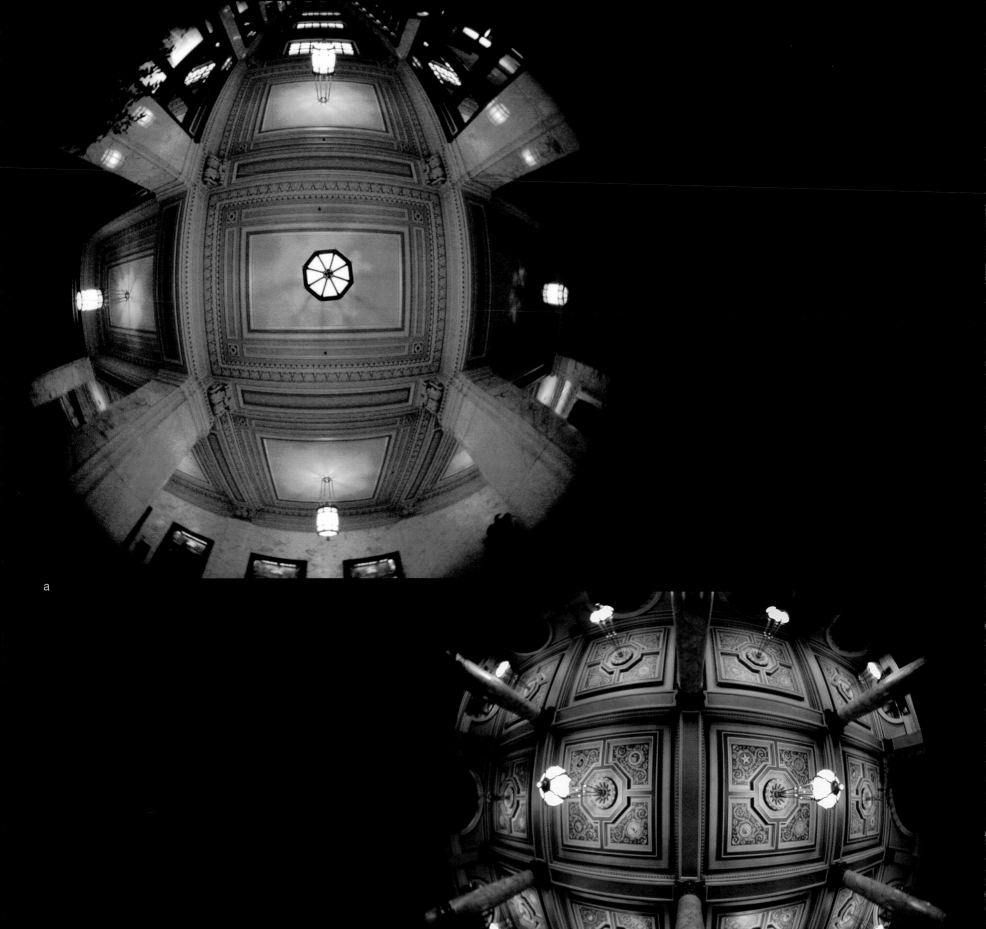

The Southern Building (a)   The Willard (b)

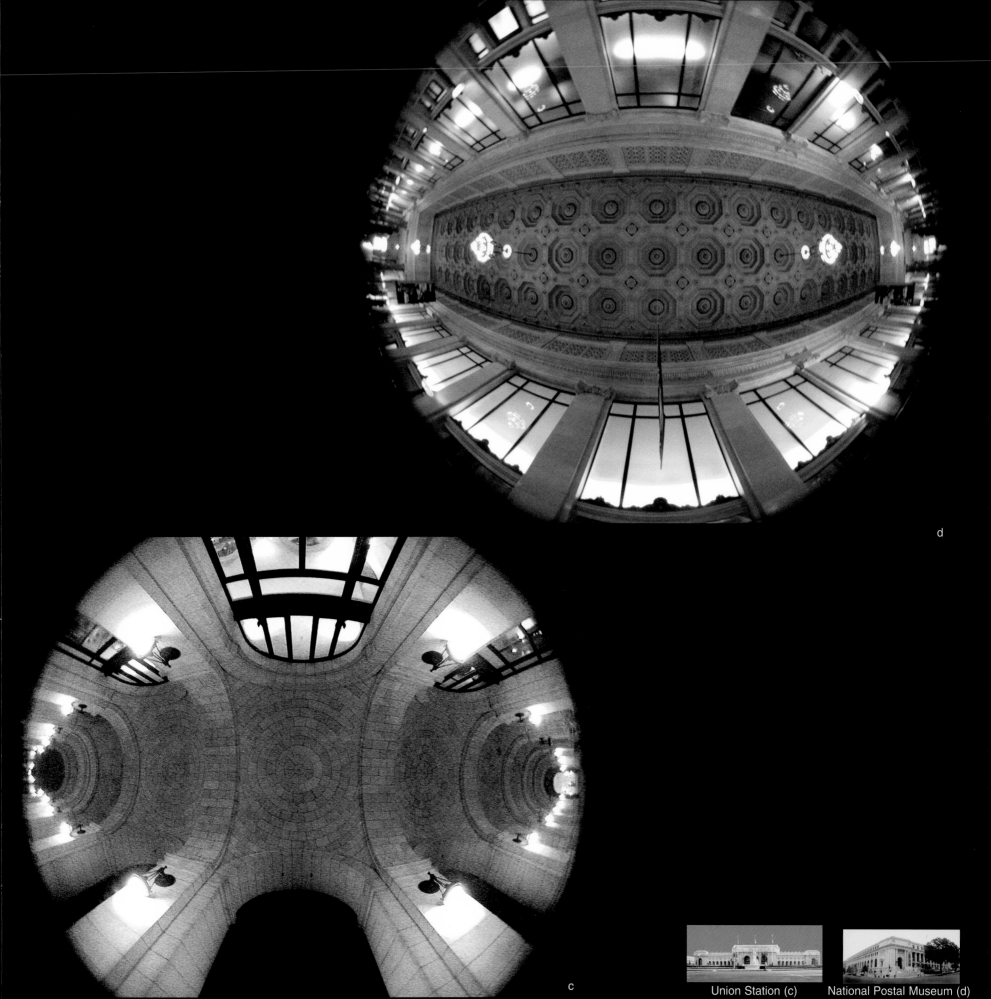

Union Station (c)    National Postal Museum (d)

a

b

c

Longworth House Office Building

Thurman Porter Building (outside & inside)

a

McPherson Building (a)

American College of
Obstetricians & Gynecologists (b)

b

c

d

World Bank (c)

International Development Bank (d)

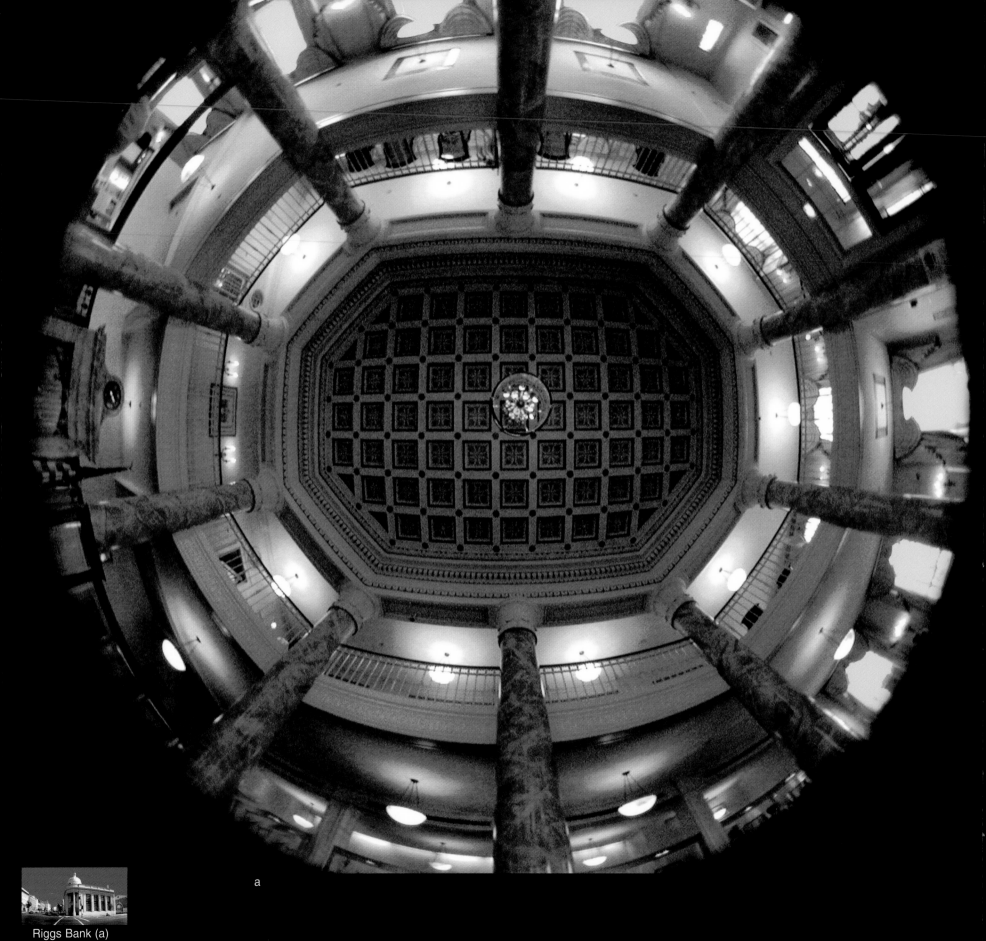

Riggs Bank (a)

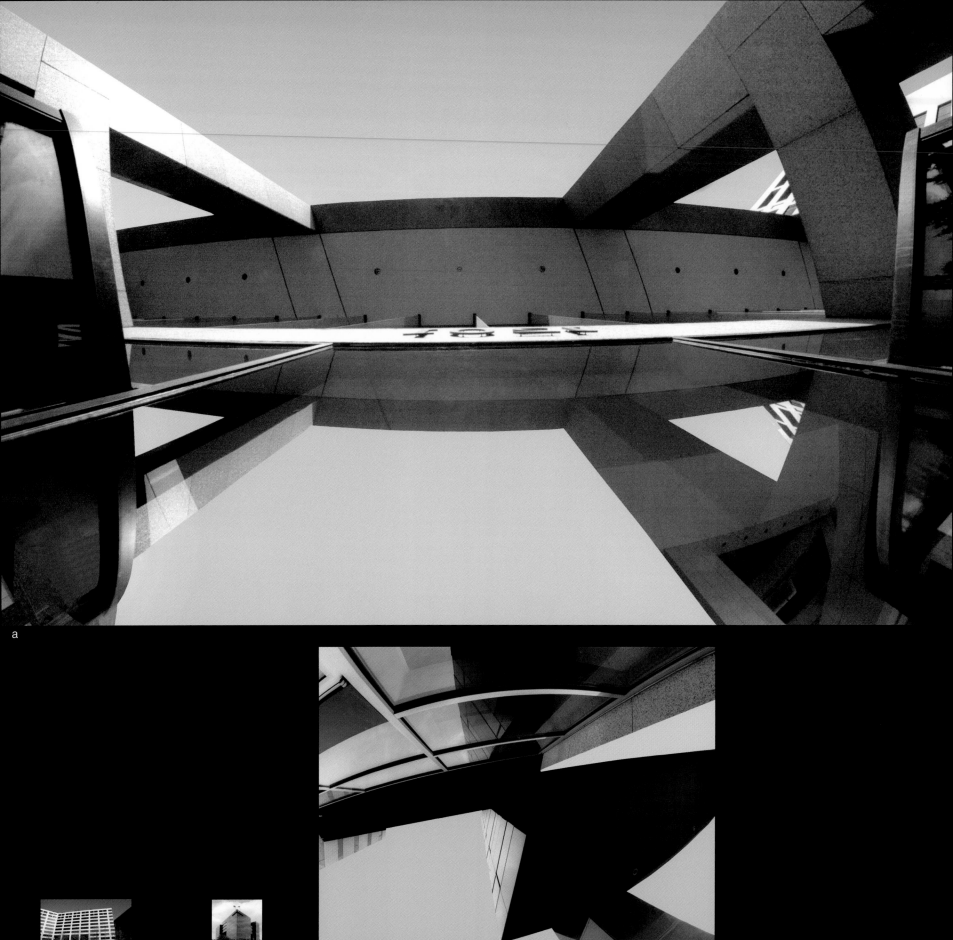

a

c

b

Cannon House Office Building (b & c)

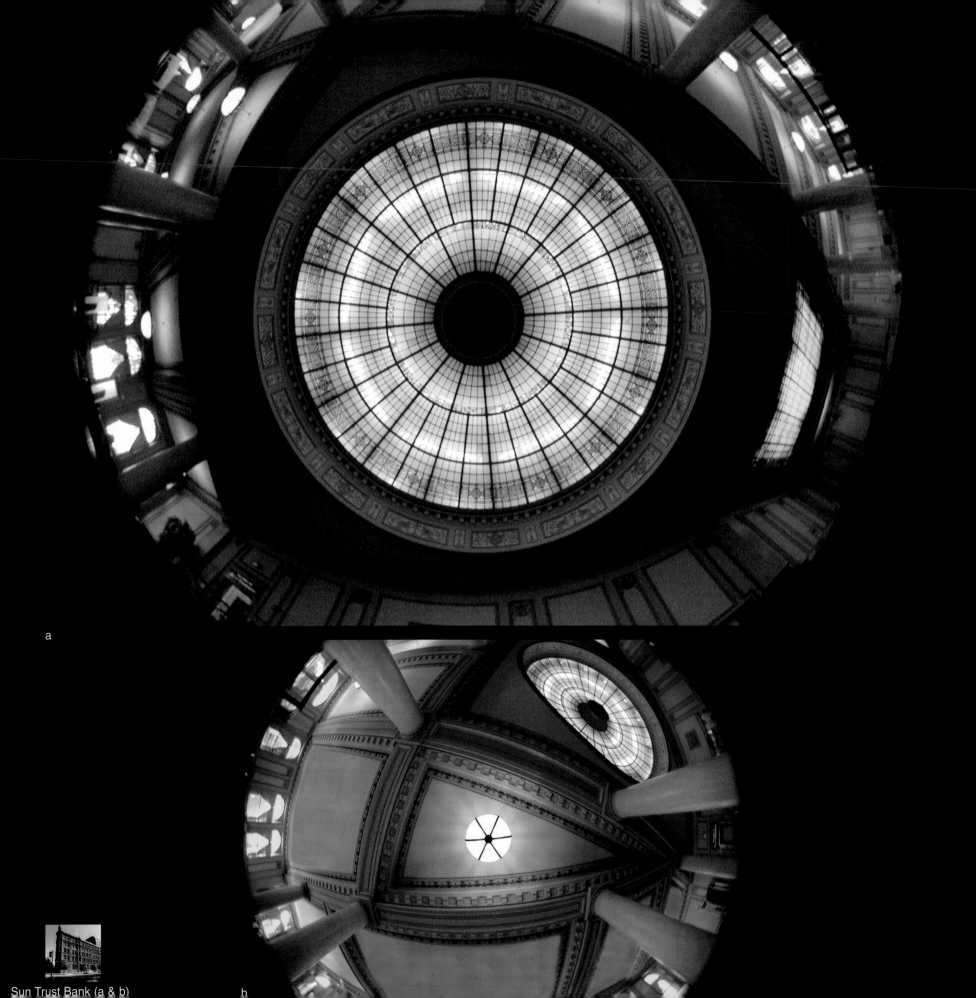

a

Sun Trust Bank (a & b)

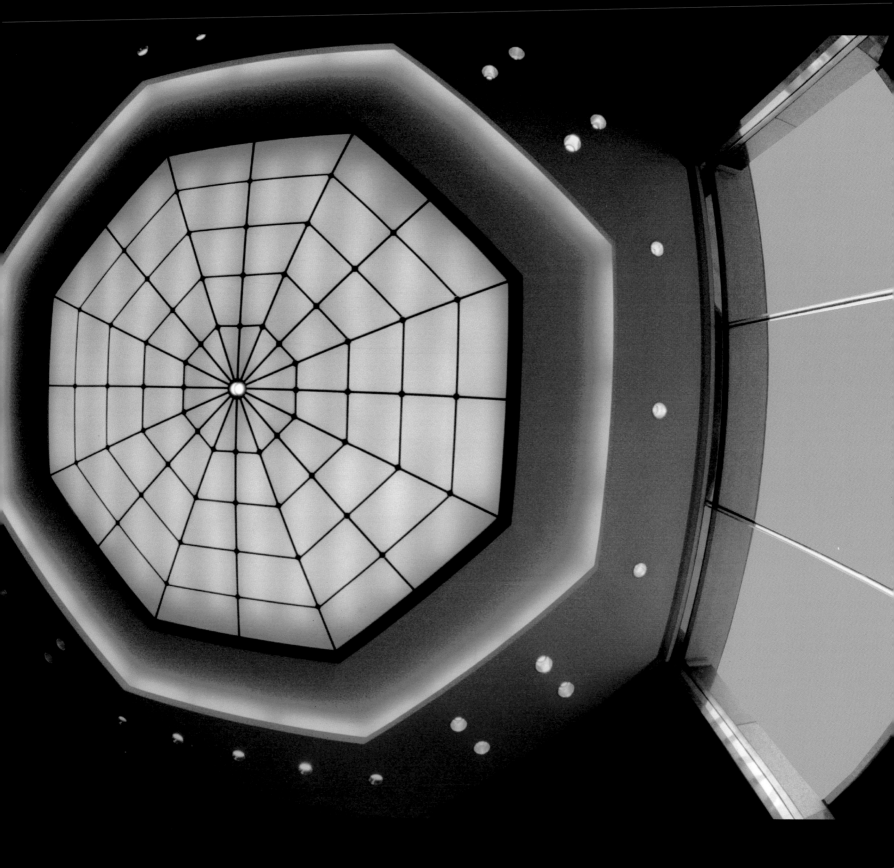

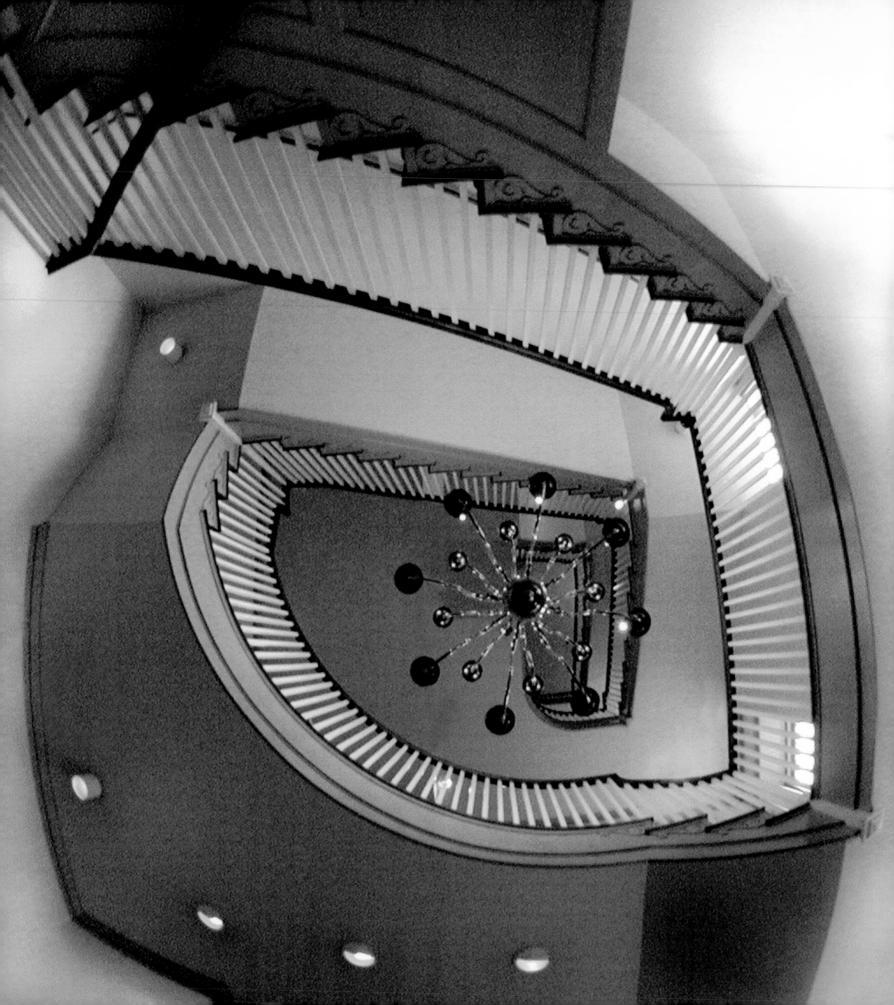

b

c

Georgetown University (a)

Russell Senate Office Building (b)

Gallaudet University (c)

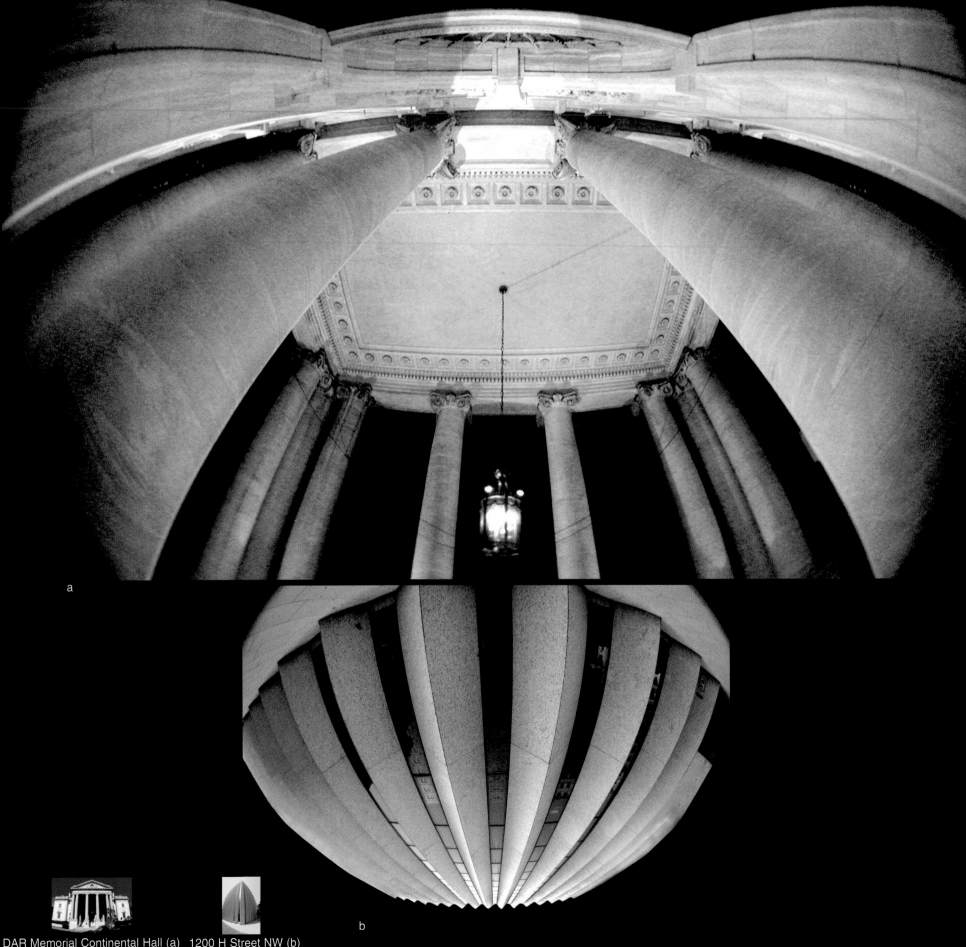

DAR Memorial Continental Hall (a)   1200 H Street NW (b)

Women's Memorial-Arlington National Cemetary

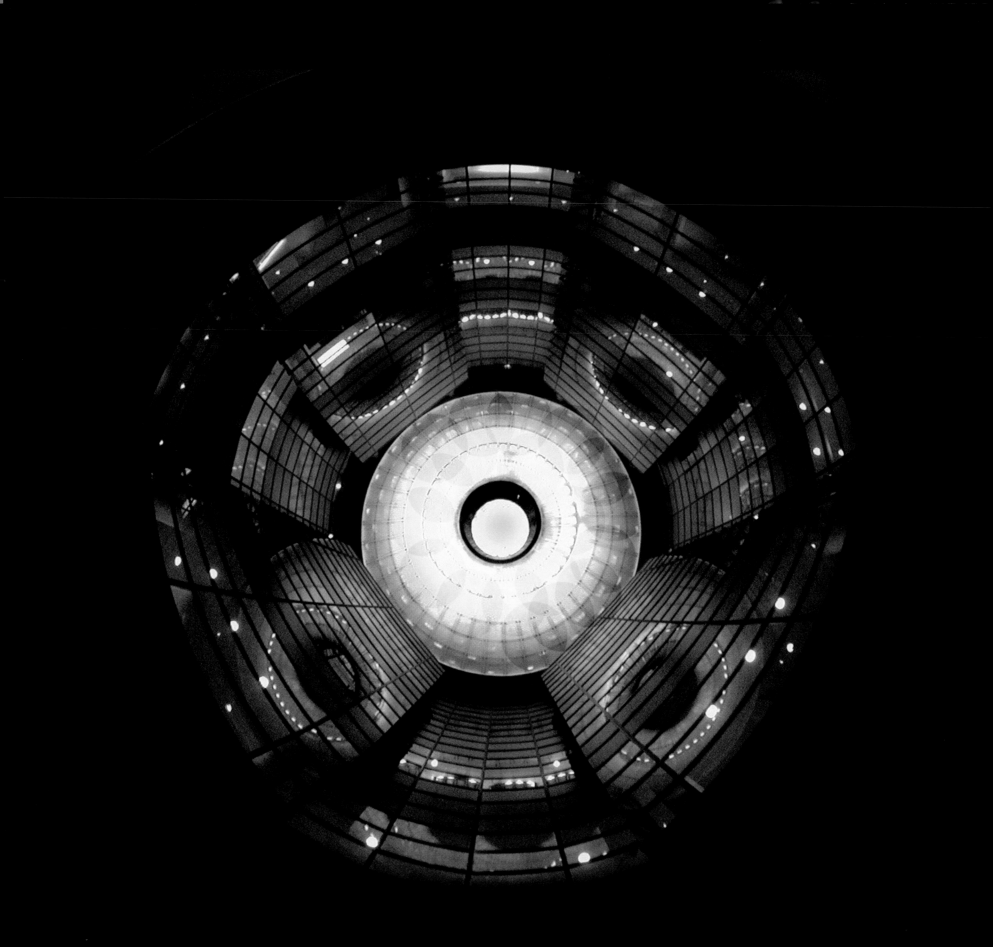

1509 K Street NW

1750 Pennsylvania Avenue NW

a

b

Georgetown University (a & b)

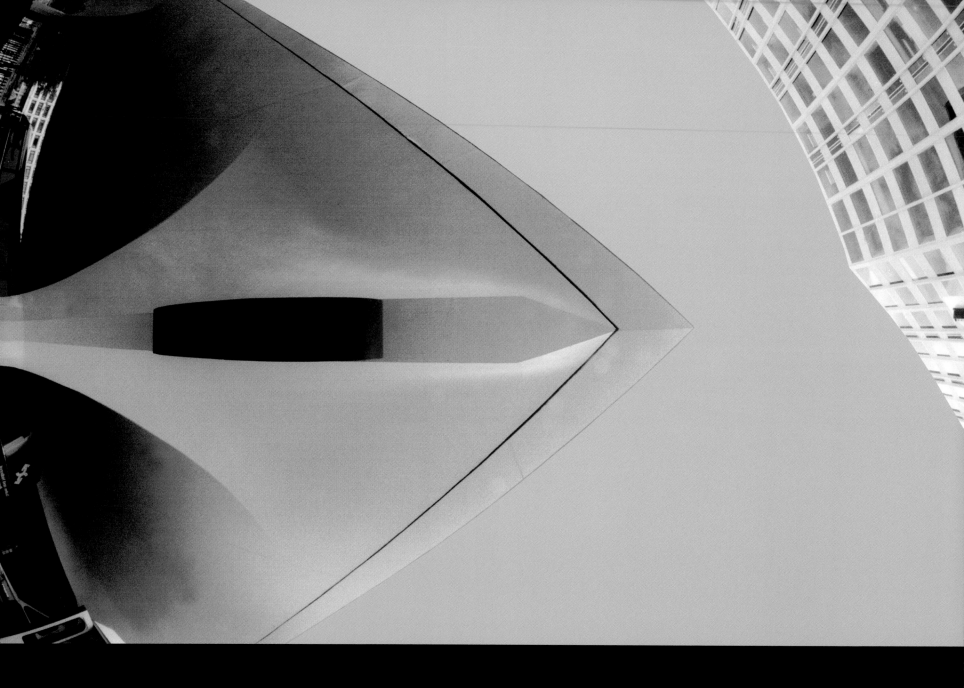

Columbia Hospital
For Women

a

b

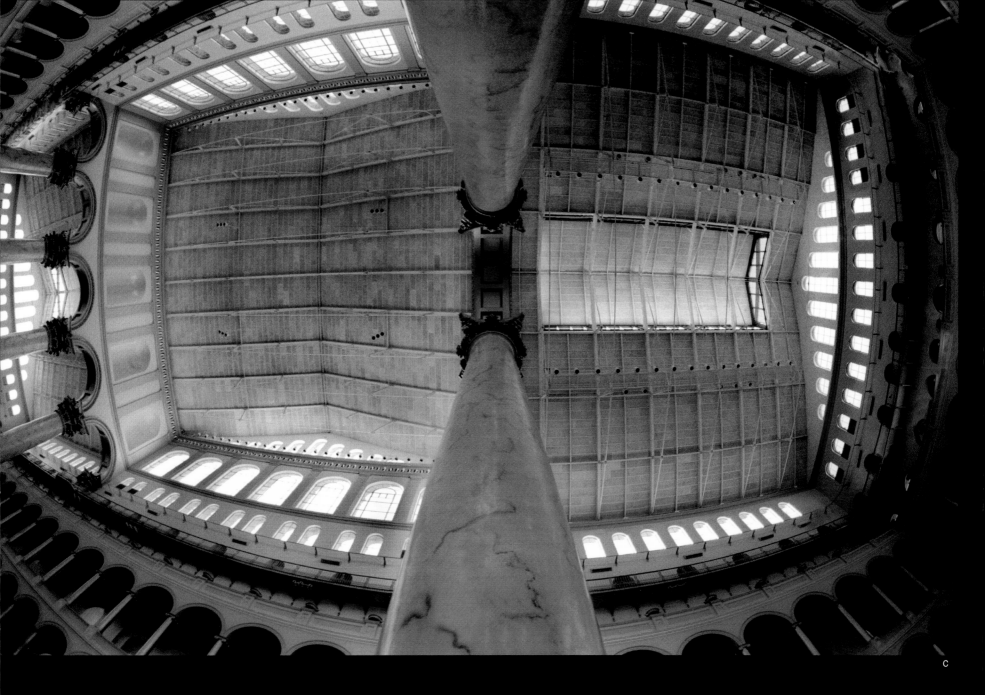

c

National Museum of Natural History (a)

National Building Museum (b & c)

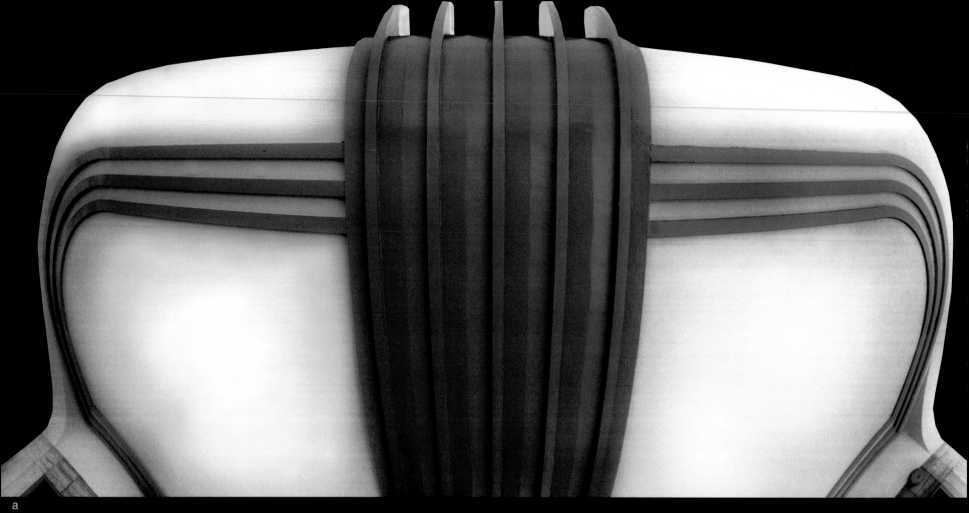

a

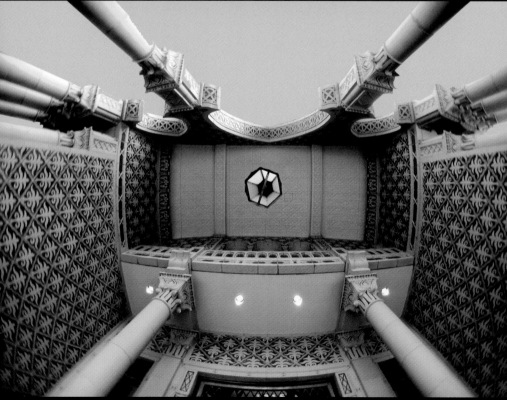

b

Old Penn Theatre (a)  Almas Shrine Temple (b)

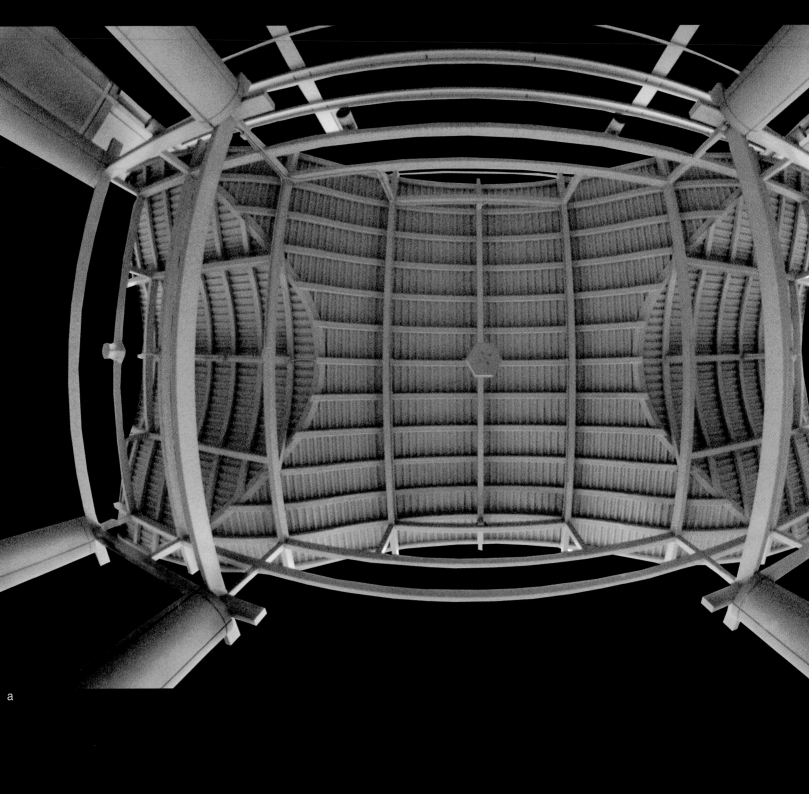

a

MCI Center (a)

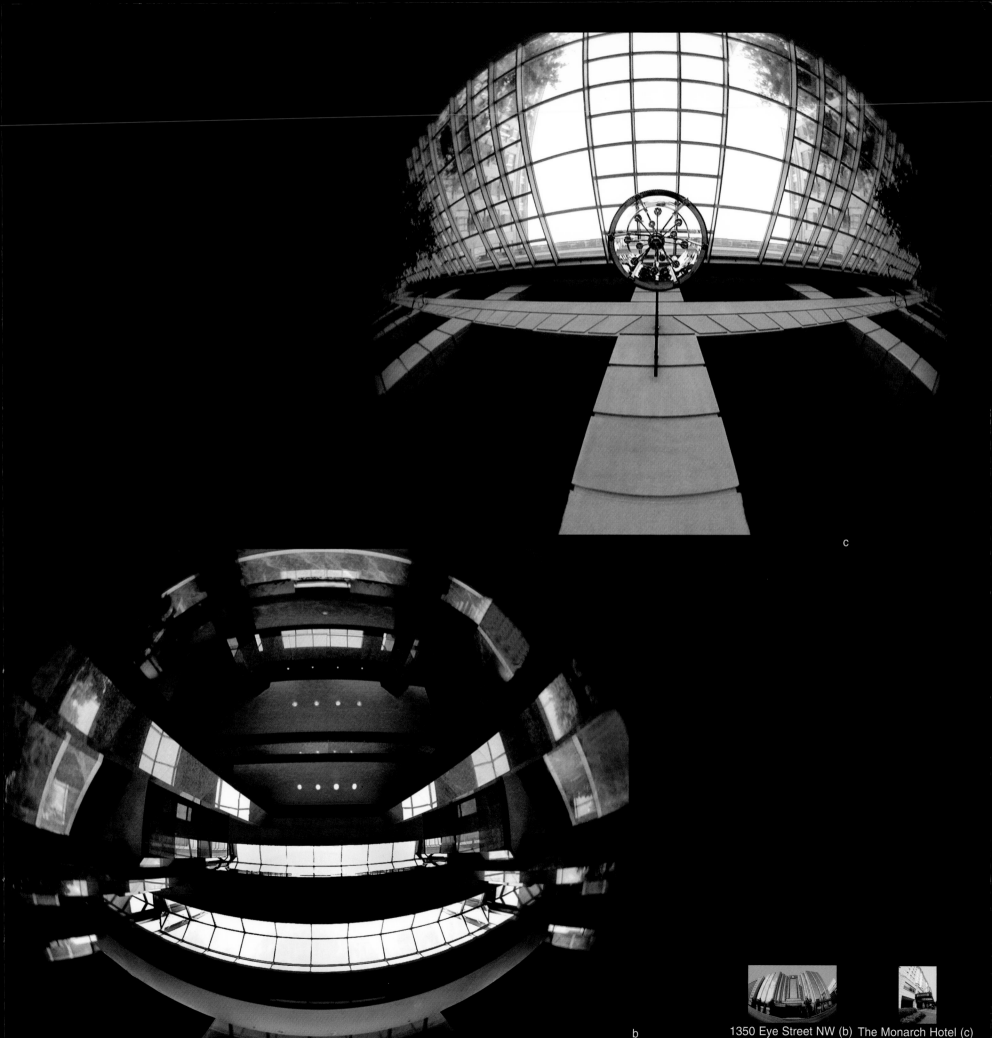

1350 Eye Street NW (b)  The Monarch Hotel (c)

a

b

1299 Pennsylvania Avenue NW (a)    Federal Reserve (b)

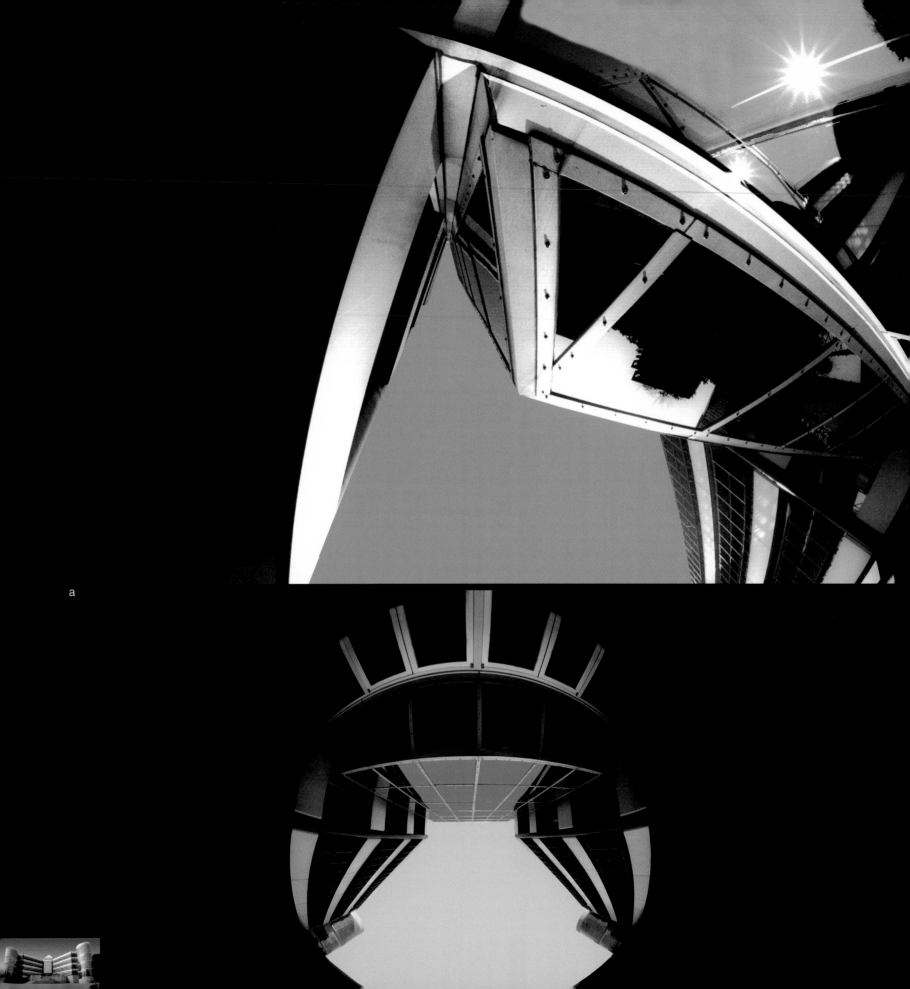

a

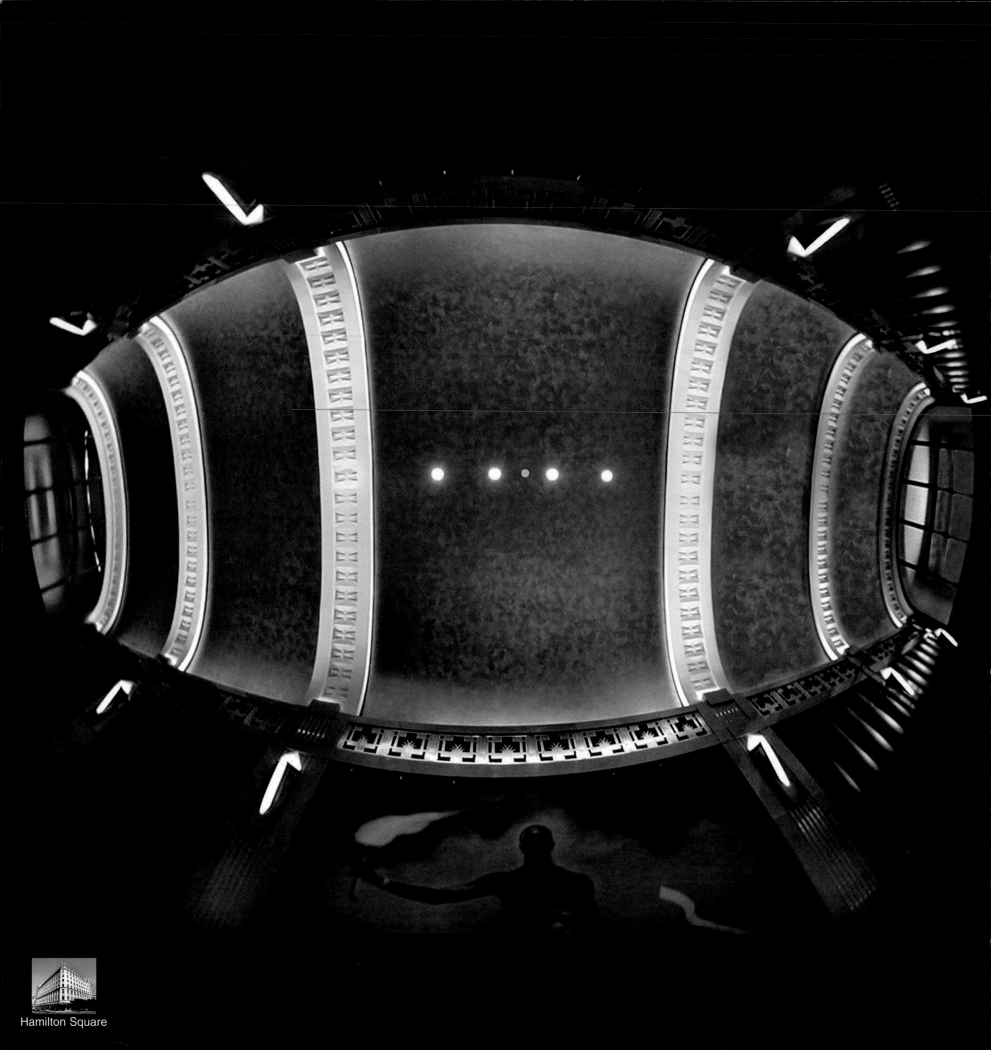

Hamilton Square

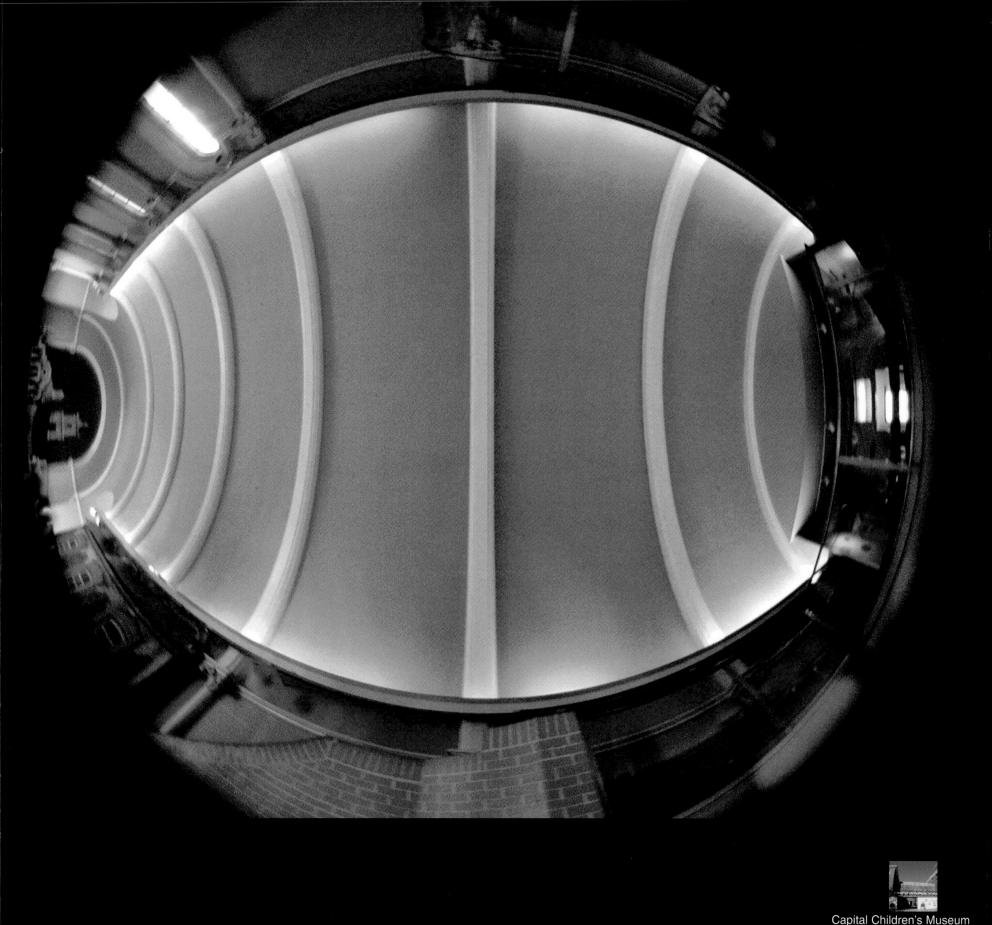

a

b

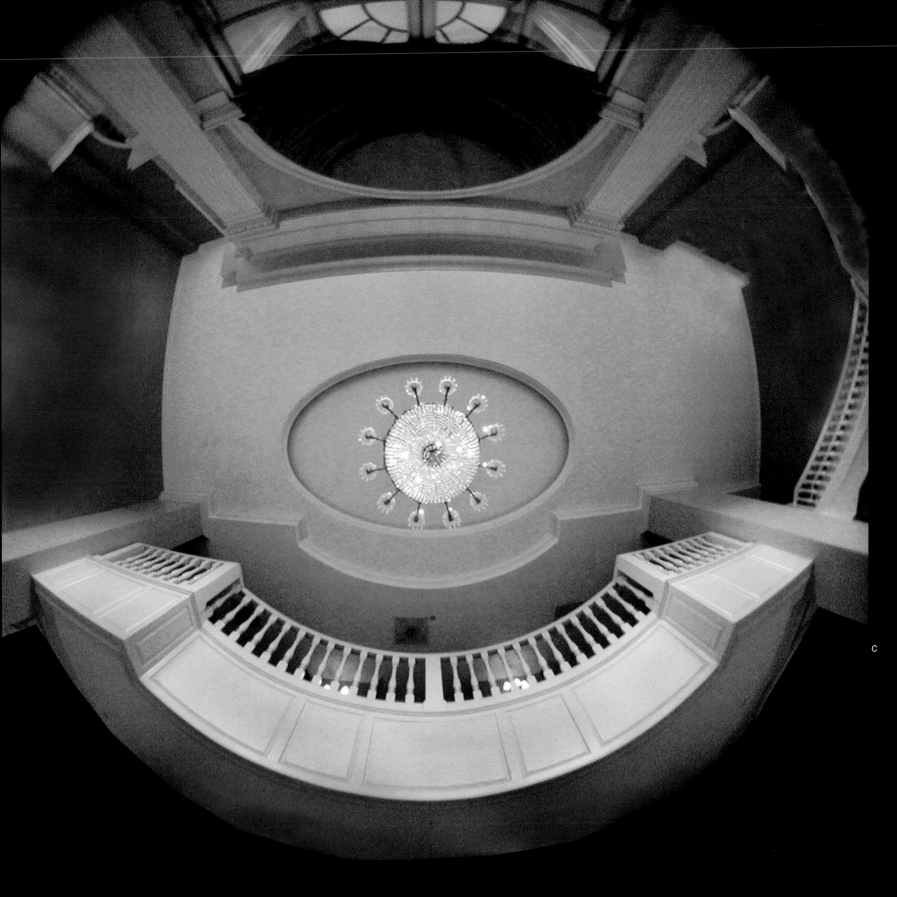

U.S. Capitol (a)   National Museum of American Art (b)   The Westin Embassy Row

a

c

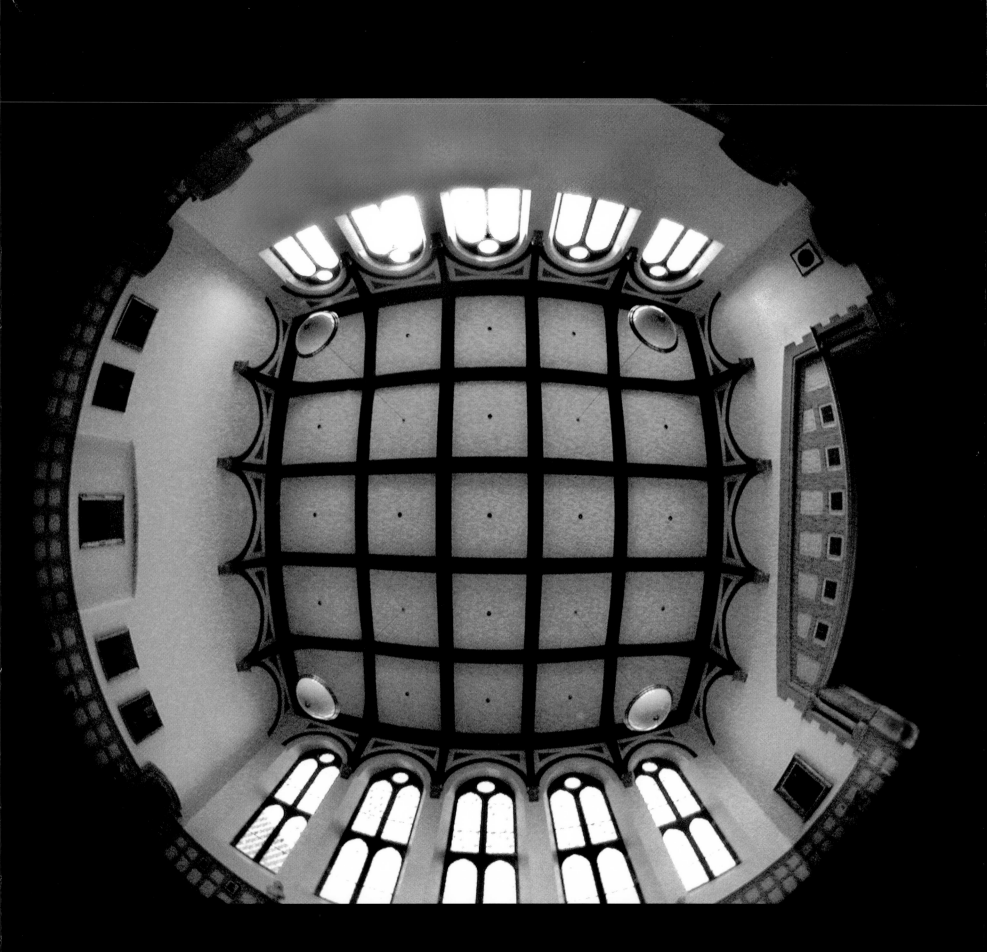

a

b

Marriott Wardman Park (a)    The Ritz Carlton (b)

c

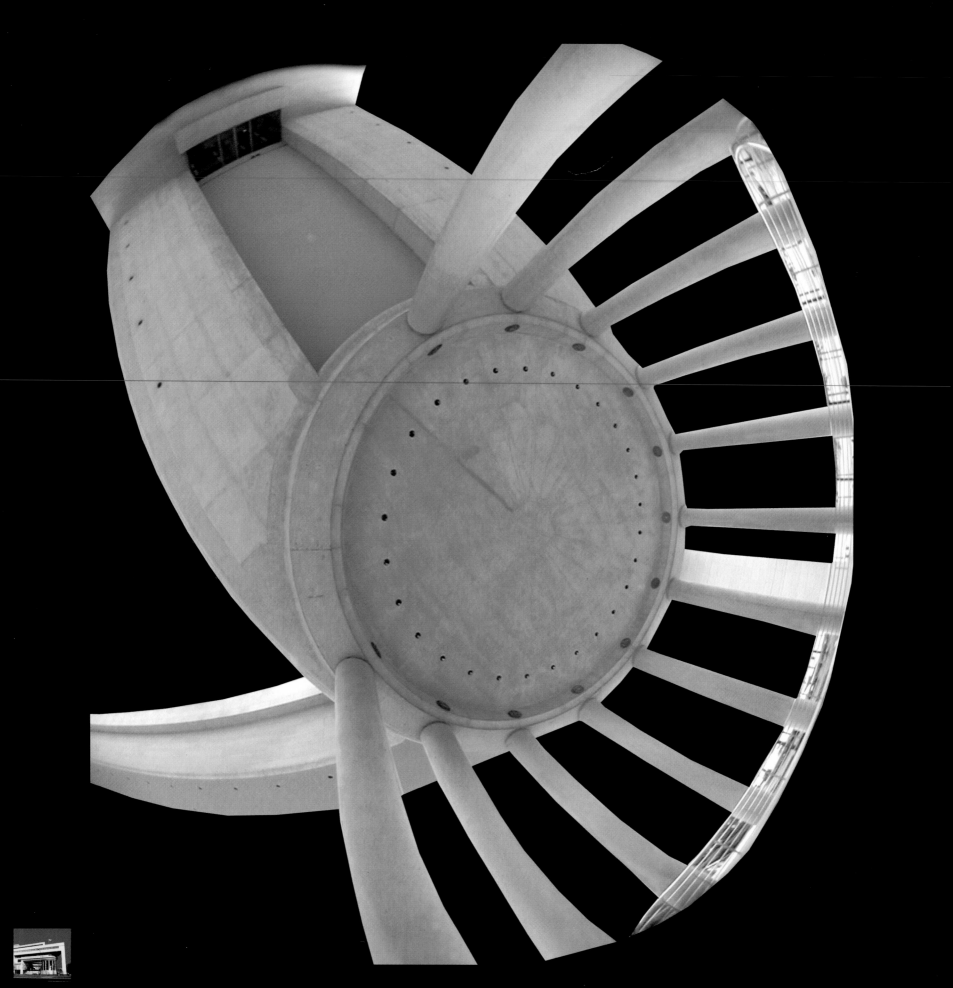

Canadian Embassy

Vietnam Memorial *(Looking Down)*

In 1982, Marty LaVor turned his hobby into a career as a full-time freelance photojournalist.

He travels extensively and has photographed in 98 countries, specializing in candid work. His photographs are used in newspapers, magazines, newsletters, corporate reports, political campaigns, posters and books. He has had 35 one-man exhibitions and his work is held in private collections throughout the world.

Marty taught himself to use a camera in 1960 when he wrote a "how to" book for hobby ceramics that became the basic instruction guide for the industry. "CERAMICS FOR ANY HANDS" contained 400 close-up photographs, had six printings and was on the market for twenty-five years.

In 1990, he produced his first photography book "NO BORDERS." It won the "Best Book Award" from the Studio Magazine International Competition and "Best in Show-Grand Prize" from the Printing Industries of Maryland. His second photography book, with over 350 photographs, documented "The VIII Plenary Session of the Theological Dialogue between the Catholic Church and the Orthodox Church", won an award from the Printing Industries of America National Competition.

He also wrote two non-photography books and has had over 100 articles published in professional journals.

Prior to his career as a professional photographer, Marty LaVor had already achieved an impressive list of personal accomplishments. He earned a Doctorate in Special Education, was an Industrial Arts teacher, a department head of a public school, the Executive Director of a rehabilitation training program for retarded and physically handicapped women, the Senior Professional for the Alabama Technical Assistance Corporation, the Senior Federal Regional Officer for the Southeast Office of Economic Opportunity, the Senior Professional Staff member for the U.S. House of Representatives Education and Labor Committee, Consultant to the U.S. Senate Committee on Aging, and Consultant to the U.S. House of Representatives Select Committee on Hunger. After he retired from the U.S. Congress he established The LaVor Group, specializing in political and public services.

❧❧❧❧❧